FRANCE

UNITED KINGDOM

BELGIUM

NL

GERMANY

LUXEM-BOURG

SWITZERLAND

ITALY

SPAIN

ANDORRA

English Channel

Calais • Dunkerque

Lille

Arras

Amiens • Saint-Quentin

Dieppe

HAUTS-DE-FRANCE

Laon

Charleville-Mézières

Metz

Haguenau

Cherbourg- Octeville

Le Havre • Rouen

Beauvais

Reims

Nancy

Strasbourg

Saint-Lô • Caen

NORMANDIE

Évreux

Argenteuil

Saint-Denis

Châlons-en-Champagne

GRAND EST

Saint-Malo

Alençon

Versailles Paris

ÎLE-DE-FRANCE

Colmar

Mulhouse

Brest

Saint-Brieuc

BRETAGNE

Laval

Chartres

Melun

Troyes

Épinal

Belfort

Quimper

Rennes

Le Mans

Orléans

Chaumont

Vesoul

Lorient

Vannes

PAYS DE LA LOIRE

Auxerre

Dijon

Besançon

Saint-Nazaire

Angers

Tours

Blois

BOURGOGNE-FRANCHE-COMTÉ

Nantes

CENTRE-VAL DE LOIRE

Bourges

Cholet

Châteauroux

Nevers

Chalon-sur-Saône

Lons-le-Saunier

Lac Léman

NORTH ATLANTIC OCEAN

Poitiers

La Roche-sur-Yon

Niort

Mâcon

La Rochelle

Limoges

Clermont-Ferrand

Bourg-en-Bresse

Annecy

Angoulême

NOUVELLE-AQUITAINE

Brive-la-Gaillarde

Saint-Étienne

Lyon

Chambéry

Périgueux

Aurillac

AUVERGNE-RHÔNE-ALPES

Grenoble

ITALY

Bordeaux

Valence

Bay of Biscay

Gap

Mont-de-Marsan

Agen

Montauban

Digne-les-Bains

Bayonne

Albi

Nîmes

PROVENCE-ALPES-CÔTE D'AZUR

Nice

Auch

Toulouse

Montpellier

Avignon

Cannes • Antibes

Pau

Tarbes

OCCITANIE

Béziers

Arles

Aix-en-Provence

Carcassonne

Sète

Marseille

Foix

Narbonne

Tarbes Toulon

Perpignan

MEDITERRANEAN SEA

Bastia

CORSE

Ajaccio

JEREMY BLACK

FRANCE

A Short History

For Charles Coutinho

On the endpapers: F. Dufour and Garnier Frères (printed by Dufrénoy),
Nouveau Paris monumental: itinéraire pratique de l'étranger dans Paris, 1878.
Library of Congress, Geography and Map Division, Washington, D.C.

First published in the United Kingdom in 2021 by
Thames & Hudson Ltd, 181A High Holborn, London WC1V 7QX

First published in the United States of America in 2021 by
Thames & Hudson Inc., 500 Fifth Avenue, New York, New York 10110

Designed by Karolina Prymaka

British Library Cataloguing-in-Publication Data
A catalogue record for this book is available from the British Library

Library of Congress Control Number 2020940725

ISBN 978-0-500-25250-5

Printed and bound in China by Toppan Leefung Printing Limited

TABLE OF CONTENTS

PREFACE

*a world of princes, and dukes and ladies of the court; I counted
above 300 coaches with 6 and 8 horses...we met the king in a
very large coach and 8 horses; there was with him the Duke and
Duchess of Burgundy and three other ladies.... Twenty miles
together all the roads were filled with vast trains of equipages.*

Meeting Louis XIV in 1699 when the royal household was moving
into winter quarters at Versailles, Richard Creed was impressed
by the scale of the magnificence. A starker reality was observed
by Robert Clive's party of tourists, who outside Toulouse in 1768,
'saw the shocking spectacle of 23 bodies of criminals which were
still fresh and exposed by the road-side. Many of them were
hanging on a gallows between four pillars, and the rest exposed
upon a wheel as they were executed.' It has always been possible
for the visitor to be faced, at any two points in time, with very
different versions of France. Country and destination, nation and
idea, France has a rich and complex history. I have set out to
show the pattern of this history, focusing on key events and with
reference to major sites, and of the development of the character
of France.

Different accounts of France's past contribute both to the
perception of the country and the extent to which that perception
is a continuing cause of controversy. For long, it was possible to
present an account of this history as an essentially unitary one,
from which there were marginal diversions, notably Vichy, when
the idea of France was more fragmented. That account, however,
looks far less certain from the perspective of today, and for several
related reasons. First, there is less of a clear sense of what France

means today given the range of politics on offer. Secondly, this range includes very different readings of French history. Thirdly, those different readings relate to a situation that has been in play for a very long time, indeed many centuries: France has a long history, and the French long memories. In Paris in 1989, to speak at a conference for the bicentenary of the Revolution, I found many lampposts covered with stickers proclaiming '*Vendée Genocide*', a reference to the Revolutionary army's brutal suppression of Royalist opposition in the Vendée in 1793–94. And now, such views are more to the fore, and are readily linked to the highly contentious nature of French politics.

This situation makes some of the popular, notably foreign, accounts of French history and, indeed, identity both bland and misleading. There can be a tendency to exaggerate support for government in any particular period, as well as to underplay signs of divisiveness. Moreover, the central narrative can underrate the extent of a dependence on conjunctures and contingencies. That is not the approach I adopt here. Instead, the emphasis will be on the unexpected nature of events and the unpredictable character of outcomes, on France as fragmented and prone to crisis. This approach ensures that the history of France is more uncertain as well as more interesting than might be appreciated, and also leads to a focus on political crises, both domestic and international. Repeatedly, indeed, the shadow of war, internal and external, lies over the history of France.

INTRODUCTION

To study the history of France means challenging above all our notion of France as a 'natural' entity, unchanged and unified over time. French scholars have long argued that geography and history are as one in helping to explain the character and development of a country. The emphasis, developed in the nineteenth-century school of French historians, is on 'possibilism', rather than 'determinism'. According to determinism, all actions arise as the result of previous actions or existing circumstances, such as geography, so an individual does not genuinely choose what to do, while possibilism allows for the effect an individual can have on the course of history. Even while accepting that history can be affected by 'possibilism', the stress in studies of the history of France remains on structures, those of geography and economic factors being the crucial ones. This approach is linked to the presentation of the *pays* as the crucial unit: a region of France in which geography and history are combined to provide a distinctive character.

France as a country now appears largely to be fronted and defined by natural boundaries – the Channel, the Atlantic, the Pyrenees, the Mediterranean, the Alps and the Rhine (although that excludes a key area of dissension, that from the Rhine to the Channel, which provided the invasion routes followed by the Germans in 1792, 1870, 1914 and 1940). The French then become those that live in the area fronted by these boundaries.

Yet, as this book will show, there was not always such fixity, no more than there was for Germany or Poland. Indeed, until the fifteenth century, the shape of France was highly uncertain, not least due to the role of the kings of England in ruling parts of France and the attempt of the dukes of Burgundy to create anew a middle state between France and Germany. Thereafter, unlike with Spain and Britain, this situation remained the case with France's frontiers, and notably its eastern frontier, until 1945. By 1550, the kingdom of France had not made the major advances to the Rhine and the Alps and in the Low Countries that were considerably to change its eastern frontier, although Henry II gained the prince-bishoprics of Metz, Toul and Verdun in 1552. The independent duchy of Savoy (a composite state with Piedmont and Nice) still reached to the River Saône until 1601 (and Savoy and Nice only became French in 1860), the English were, until 1558, in Calais (and in 1544–50 in Boulogne), and the Habsburgs in Alsace, Artois and Franche-Comté until 1648, 1659, and 1678 respectively, while Lorraine was an independent duchy until 1766.

It is all too easy to assume that expansion to France's subsequent frontiers was inevitable, not least because we tend to associate states historically with the modern shape of countries; but this is misleading. Indeed, French expansion took it into regions never hitherto ruled as part of France, as with Corsica in 1768. Moreover, much of the expansion was into what had been part of the middle kingdom created in the ninth century from the Frankish inheritance. In the fifteenth century, much of this had been given international vitality as an expanding state by the dukes of Burgundy. Subsequently, a large part of the Burgundian inheritance had been acquired by the Habsburgs, notably the Emperor Charles V (r. 1519–1556) and, later, his son Philip II of Spain (r. 1556–1598). As a result, the struggle between Habsburg and Valois, Spain and France, was, in part, a conflict between Burgundy and France that, in turn, continued a long-established struggle.

To many Germans, any eastward French expansion was not immutable but, rather, the product of French strength that could be reversed. Ultimately, indeed, French hegemony over the lands between the rivers Saône and Marne, on the one hand, and the Rhine, on the other, depended on military strength, for the dukes of Lorraine were traditional Habsburg allies, in effect heirs to the position of the dukes of Burgundy. Moreover, there was opposition in Germany to prevent the consolidation of the position France had acquired in Alsace in 1648 thanks to the Peace of Westphalia, a consolidation that was not settled until 1793. The position in Alsace led Louis XIV (r. 1643–1715) to press for eastward expansion in order to link up his possessions. Diplomacy, which resulted in the French gain of Lorraine by inheritance in 1766 (in fulfilment of a treaty of 1738), and force, which led to that of Strasbourg in 1681, and to occupations of Lorraine, as in 1733, were crucial on the eastern frontier. In turn, the Germans held most of Alsace and part of Lorraine anew in 1871–1918 and 1940–45. Separately, French governmental systems as a whole fell as a result of successful invasions in 1814, 1815, 1870 and 1940. In addition, over a longer time span, the nature of statehood changed greatly, and, with it, assumptions about how territorialization should be treated.

Moreover, within France, there was contestation over politics and religion – as well as in other spheres, notably social relations – for much of the last half-millennium. This strife may seem distant today to tourists eating Gascon fare or visiting one-time Protestant strongholds, such as La Rochelle, but it has a strong grip on the past and the imagination, and sometimes echoes into attitudes in the present, as in the Vendée on the western coast.

War is important to the history of France, a point that underlines the display of military strength in Paris every Bastille Day. The nation, its communities and its families all have war in their background. At the same time, it can be all too easy in discussing both the war and the history to underplay the human cost. Jean Martin de La Colonie recalled of the response to a British attack in 1704:

> We were all fighting hand to hand, hurling them back as they clutched at the parapet; men were slaying, or tearing at the muzzles of guns and the bayonets which pierced their entrails; crushing under their feet their own wounded comrades, and even gouging out their opponent's eyes with their nails, when the grip was so close that neither could use their weapons.

Civilians also suffered. In 1815, Major William Turner wrote: 'Every town and village is completely ransacked and pillaged by the Prussians and neither wine, spirits or bread are to be found. The whole country from the frontier to Paris has been laid waste by the march of troops.' This devastation was seen as a response to the harsh treatment of the German lands by French forces from 1792. Alongside the reparations enforced on France in 1815 and 1871, and the serious wartime damage in 1914–18, this behaviour helped explain the reparations demanded from Germany in 1919 and the occupation of the Ruhr in 1923, although that background tends to be forgotten. The devastation of war and the many hardships entailed are a reality of history that should not be concealed beneath a blizzard of dates, and this devastation makes the historical architectural richness of France today surprising.

War, a key aspect of politics, underlined the deficiencies of environmental determinism – whereby the form of a country, and therefore a nation, is prescribed by physical geography. Moreover, regionally based historical geography, that of the *pays*, placed less of an emphasis on the environment as a determining force and more on its interaction with human society, an emphasis particularly associated with Paul Vidal de La Blache (1845–1918), who was appointed to the chair of geography at the Sorbonne in 1899. Arguing that the environment was a context for human development rather than the central issue in history, the emphasis was therefore shifted back to humanity, to the varieties of human activity, to cultural geography, and to the complexities of nation building. Furthermore, greater weight could be placed on influences from outside the locality, as in Vidal de La Blache's *Tableau de la géographie de la France* (1903). Seven years later, he published an article suggesting a new division of the French regions based on the fields of influence of large urban centres, a view of the human environment that did not centre on physical geography.

Vidal de La Blache's work was taken up by Lucien Febvre (1878–1956), who was suspicious of the use of the notion of influences and, instead, preferred the idea of an interaction between man and environment. Febvre argued that distinctive *genres de vie* (ways of life) existed in specific regions, and that their variation was greater than that in physical geography. To explain this situation required the fusion of history with geography as part of a multi-disciplinary character of history. In fulfilment of this, a series of officially sponsored French regional historical atlases appeared from 1969 to 1979, before falling victim to budgetary issues.

There were certainly major variations in government within France prior to the attempt under the Revolution to introduce national systematization, including important distinctions in taxation between the different types of local administrative areas known as the *pays d'élection* and the *pays d'état*, and of law between the region of customary (feudal) law and that of written (Roman) law, as well as between jurisdictions. To this day, the Channel Islands retain the organization of local administration that dates from the French *ancien régime* (the 'old rule', the name given to the political system of France from around the fifteenth century to the Revolution in 1789).

There were also major internal distinctions within France in terms of customs, especially between the region of the *cinq grosses fermes* (the 'five large farms' that covered much of the northern half of France) and the *provinces réputées étrangères* (the so-called 'foreign-deemed provinces' that covered much of the south). Taxation was also an issue, with the country divided in terms of the crucial salt tax between the regions of the *grande gabelle*, the *petite gabelle*, the *gabelle du Rethel*, the *gabelle du saline* and the *quart-bouillon*, as well as the redeemed provinces and the free provinces. The diverse nature of administration, without uniformity in taxation, local laws and local government, both reflected and encouraged a sense of regional identity. Contemporaries held the ideas of such boundaries clearly in mind, for the consequences could be costly, as in the extensive *pays de grande gabelle*, where a fixed minimum annual amount of salt had to be purchased irrespective of need. To distinguish these zones, Jacques Necker, the finance minister, published the *Carte des gabelles* (1781).

The accretional character of the French state was reflected in such arrangements. 'France' described the patrimony of a ruling dynasty whose possessions and pretensions extended as feudal overlordships, rather than an area bounded by 'natural' linear frontiers, such as rivers. For example, in the extensive negotiations from 1697 until the mid-eighteenth century with the prince-bishopric of Liège over Bouillon, which France had annexed in 1678, references were made to the eleventh century, and fantastic genealogies, legendary medieval tales and ancient authors who based their comments on hearsay all played a major role.

That situation changed from the 1750s, as borders were rectified in order to remove enclaves by a process of exchange. Moreover, the Treaty of Turin of 1760 between France and Savoy-Piedmont settled the Alpine boundary on the basis of the watershed and incorporated eight maps, which marked a replacement of earlier methods of frontier negotiation. The shaping of a more precise border was an aspect of the formation of modern France.

All this shows that, far from the unitary concept of the imagination, France was a diverse group of regions in geographic, cultural and administrative terms that only slowly evolved into what we now deem to be a 'nation'. Indeed, the boundaries and governmental patterns of modern France are a misleading guide to the history of the lands that became France.

1. Prehistoric Legacies

The 2,753 Standing Stones of Carnac, prehistoric monuments dating from 6,600 years ago in Brittany, remain a striking image of ancient France (see pl. 1). The cave paintings of animals in Lascaux, made about 17,000 years ago, also famous and again a source of impressive photographs, alas are not so visible: closed in 1963, they have to be seen through the effective Lascaux II reconstruction.

Archaeological finds abound across France and deserve more attention than many tourists give to them. These finds are aspects of an ancient past that has provided images, mythic or otherwise, that stretch to the present. In particular, the tribes of what became France, going back to some of the inhabitants of the present country before the Romans arrived in the first century BCE, retain a pull on the national consciousness. Indeed, many of these tribes remain with us today in the names of regions, and in the characteristics called upon by the people that lay claim to their legacy.

The last Ice Age was important to France's history, although it was, in practice, a series of ice advances with intervening warmer periods, and even when the ice advanced, most of France was not covered. Evidence of human settlement in this period has been found. Alongside Neanderthals, there were hominids. The Musée de la Préhistoire des gorges du Verdon suggests there has been human life in that region from about 400,000 years ago. Cave systems, notably in the Dordogne region, south-western France, provide evidence of human life – in the form of anatomically modern humans – about 32,000 years ago, and the paintings reflect the focus on animals to be expected in hunter-gatherer societies. As part of a changing system of nomenclature, Cro-Magnon, a rock shelter in the Vézère Valley of the Dordogne, where human remains were discovered in 1868 by diggers preparing a new rail link, gave the name to what are now generally termed European early modern humans, those from about 48,000 to about 15,000 years ago. Their skeletons reveal a hard life, one of injury and infection, but also suggest cognitive development to a level that permitted rituals. Cro-Magnon remains in that area are extensive, including prehistoric camps near Les Eyzies and the pictures of animals that can be seen in the Abri de Cap Blanc and the Font-de-Gaume and Combarelles grottoes. The focus on illustrations of animals can also be seen in prehistoric caves in the Pyrenees, notably at Niaux and Bédeilhac, and in the Massif Central, as at Chauvet-Pont d'Arc.

The warmer weather that followed the Last Glacial Maximum, which ended about 16,000 years ago, caused a major rise in the sea level, by about 100 to 120 metres. This led to a retreat of the coastline, to the creation of *la Manche*/the Channel, and to the abandonment of some cave systems. The warmer weather also encouraged the spread northwards of more vigorous plant and animal life and, in time, the humans, who followed about 15,000 years ago, developed both cultivation and pastoralism. That was the basis for the Lascaux cave dwellings and for the Megalithic Stone Age settlements, as at Carnac, Locmariaquer and Gavrinis in Brittany. The stone alignments were probably for astronomical reasons, linked to ritual practices. Flint mines were of importance and, in Vassieux-en-Vercors in the Drôme department, the Musée de la Préhistoire de Vassieux en Vercors is on the site of one.

Visible even from the sea and dominating a huge area as the symbol of a very organized society, the tumulus of Saint Michel on the edge of Carnac, at 125 metres (410 feet) long and 10 metres (33 feet) high, may have been one of the largest stone structures in the world about 7,000 years ago. Even in the Neolithic period, the extent of trade networks was impressive, with stones at Carnac coming from as far as Portugal and the Baltic. Later pottery designs of the Bronze Age confirm the links that ran across Europe. Long before the Celts, there were some sophisticated cultural goods, and France was no backwater but part of the wider world.

The transformative diffusion of metals is grouped first in the Bronze Age, and then, from about 500 BCE in France, the Iron Age. Iron axes and ploughs made it easier to clear the woodland and to work the soil. Indeed, alongside the retention of significant areas of woodland, large parts of lowland France were swept of trees during the Iron Age. This opened up what became a permanent difference between upland and lowland France, one that was linked to a significant contrast in the density of population.

In what became France, archaeologists have distinguished a number of cultures, particularly the Hallstatt from about 900 BCE, and the Celts from about 500 BCE, although there was a degree of overlap, and notably between the last two. At the Gallic Bibracte in today's Nièvre department, there is the Musée de la civilisation Celtique. The Celts, more specifically La Tène culture, had a number of territories that were centred on fortified hilltop towns ruled over by princes. These towns were the foci of trade networks that in part supplied Greek bases in southern France, notably Massalia (Marseille), which was founded in about 600 BCE, Nice and Agathe, and therefore fed Mediterranean trade. Other coastal bases included Antipolis, Olbia and Tauroeis between Nice and Marseille, Emporion near later Narbonne and Alalia on the Corsican coast. The Greeks moved north from the Mediterranean, notably building a settlement at Glanum near Saint-Rémy-de-Provence. Subsequently, the Romans took over the town. The excavations of a Celtic settlement can be visited at the Oppidum d'Entremont just north of Aix.

The Celts of what became France were known by the Romans as Gauls, although their territories extended further than the boundaries of modern France. In his *Gallic Wars* (58–49 BCE), Julius Caesar noted the diversity of Gaul and its division among different tribes. The Gauls had a rich civilization, one that was capable of producing art of some sophistication, as with the Treasure of Vix in the museum at Châtillon-sur-Seine in Burgundy, a collection of finds from the tomb of a Celtic woman buried in a chariot. Impressive pottery and swords were produced by a society that was able to use metals and was knowledgeable about agriculture. Indeed, even from the critical comments of the Romans, it is clear to see that they were impressed by the Celts.

2. Roman France

Move down into the valley of the River Gardon and look up at the Pont du Gard (see pl. II), the dramatic first-century CE aqueduct carrying water to the nearby city of Nemasus (Nîmes). The three tiers of arches were a triumph of purpose and skill, and the quality of the museum increases the appeal of the site. Yet, war was the key to the establishment of Roman control. Attacking Massalia (Marseille) in 49 BCE when it backed one of his Roman opponents, Julius Caesar blockaded the port and then, in order to help compress the soil for a mighty ramp, 'all the woods were felled'. Two towers on rollers were placed on the ramp, and from there fire was directed at the defenders. The catapults of the attackers bombarded the towers, while, in turn, the attacking troops were pummelled by stones dropped from the walls. Inexorable effort won Caesar success. Having conquered the Celts of northern Italy, which they termed Cisalpine (this side of the Alps) Gaul, the Romans had sought to expand their power into Transalpine Gaul, establishing control over much of southern France in 125–121 BCE, notably by beating the Saluvii tribe at their capital, Entremont, in about 123–122 BCE. In part, this expansion was to protect Massalia, which had earlier backed Rome against Carthage. However, in reality, the extension of Roman power, not least to establish a land route to the wealthy provinces in Spain, was the key theme, and this extension was anchored by the establishment of fortresses such as Aquae Sextiae, now Aix-en-Provence.

The pursuit of power was certainly the central goal for Julius Caesar, who became the provincial governor of northern Italy and southern France in 59 BCE. The following year, in response to an invasion of Germanic tribes, he expanded his power northwards, beating the tribes piecemeal, and, in 56 BCE, conquered Brittany, defeating the Veneti in a naval battle. The year 52 BCE was key in terms of conflict. Caesar then faced stronger resistance, particularly organized by Vercingétorix of the Arverni tribe, who brought a measure of unity among the Gauls, but, aside from divisions among the Gauls, they had to face Caesar's brutal and remorseless methods and the more disciplined fighting style of the Romans. Caesar's deputy, Titus Labienus, defeated the Parisii, who had backed Vercingétorix's rising in the battle of Lutetia in what is now Paris. Meanwhile, Vercingétorix was unable to relieve Avaricum (Bourges) when Caesar besieged it, but his scorched-earth tactics helped lead to the supply problems that contributed to the failure of Caesar's siege of Gergovia, a formidable position.

At Alesia, Vercingétorix made what became his last stand on a hilltop town, which Caesar surrounded with a ditch and earthworks. Breakout attempts to avoid being starved out were defeated. A relief force failed to penetrate the outward fortified line of contravallation that protected the besiegers from relief, lines that were important to Roman siegecraft as the attempted relief of positions was a key element in the fighting of the period. Vercingétorix surrendered, and was imprisoned until presented in Caesar's triumph in Rome in 46 BCE, after which he was strangled. The site of Alesia is dominated by a bronze statue of Vercingétorix, a product of Napoleon III's attempt to demonstrate a pre-Roman origin for France. A divided tribal opposition to Roman conquest was presented as the valorous resistance of a Gaulish nation. The defeat had been bad, but France was given a hero, and France entered civilization – in the sense of Roman civilization – which for Napoleon III, looking in retrospect, was an excellent thing.

Thereafter – despite the idea offered in the popular *Astérix* comic-book stories, created by René Goscinny and appearing from 1959, of heroic resistance in remote fastnesses – the Roman perspective was that Gaul was held with relative ease. Thus the fortified frontier of Roman control became the Rhine; this established a key divide between Gaul and the Germanic peoples that would become important to the later cultural and political identity of France.

The Romans ruled all of Gaul but it was not one territory. Instead, Gaul was divided into a number of provinces. Most of Gaul was in Gallia Lugdunensis, but some was in Belgica, and some in Aquitania. Lugdunum (Lyon) became the political capital of Gaul and, until the third century CE, its economic capital, too. Gaul was valuable, providing goods for Italy, including wine, ceramics, metal goods and, from the Camargue, salt. Gaul, in turn, received from the Romans the template of control and civilization, at least as understood and enforced by the Romans. While existing towns adapted to the Roman model, many cities, indeed the basis of the modern city system, were founded on this model and administered as Roman centres in order to foster the Romanization of Gaul. Major cities included Gallia Narbonensis (Narbonne), Tolosa (Toulouse), Burdigala (Bordeaux), Augustodunum (Autun), Mediolanum Santonum (Saintes) and Lapurdum (Bayonne).

These cities gained the temples, amphitheatres and forums that characterized Roman cities in the Mediterranean, and much of their remains can still be seen. Triumphal arches from the period include the Porte de Mars in Reims, while the amphitheatre in Paris, the Arènes de Lutèce, is of interest. It was destroyed during 'Barbarian' attacks at the end of the third century, as were the major public baths, the remains of which are an impressive

part of the Musée de Cluny in Paris. The remains of the baths in
Metz can be seen in the local museum; Autun displays extensive
remains including a substantial theatre and two gates; while
Saintes has an amphitheatre and the Arc de Germanicus. There
are more dramatic Roman remains in the south, especially in
Arles, and in Nîmes with its amphitheatre, Maison Carrée and
Porte d'Auguste. One of the best preserved, Nîmes's amphitheatre is extraordinary for the quality of its design, sightlines and
accessibility. Orange has a well-preserved Roman theatre, which
included a statue of Augustus as well as a stage wall facing the
seats, and also a Roman triumphal arch. A Roman town can be
approached through the excavations at Vaison-la-Romaine.

The cities were linked by roads and bridges, fragments of
which can be seen west of Nîmes on the Via Domitia, the route
from Italy, crossing the Alps by the Col de Montgenèvre, to Spain.
The Romans built about 21,000 kilometres (13,000 miles) of roads
in Gaul. Marcus Vipsanius Agrippa, who reorganized Gaul under
the Emperor Augustus, developed a network of Via Agrippas
from Lugdunum. One led travellers to Boulogne, from where
ships sailed to Britannia (Britain), while another went from
Lugdunum to Colonia Agrippina (Cologne). Other roads marched
alongside the rivers, for example from Massalia to Lugdunum, or
filled in gaps in the river system, for example the Via Aquitania
joining Gallia Narbonensis to Burdigala, and roads that joined
Lutetia to the Loire Valley, and Lugdunum to Mediolanum
Santonum. This system of roads showed a key aspect of the significance of Gaul to the Romans: it provided crucial backing to
the territories in Britain and the Rhineland.

Alongside the settlement of Roman colonists on the land there
were practised methods designed to placate the Gauls and to
incorporate them into the Roman system. Tribal leaders took part
in a process of Romanization, notably with the spread of Roman

religious cults, and of the Latin language; and with the enticement of the benefits of citizenship. Recruitment into the army was also a crucial form of social mobility and political integration, helping indeed to create a 'Gallo-Roman' spirit. As in Britain and Spain, Romanization was more apparent in some areas than others, thus in the Rhône Valley, rather than in Brittany. In the former, 30 kilometres (19 miles) south of Lyon, one of the most important archaeological sites in Europe, the Musée Gallo-romain de Saint-Romain-en-Gal-Vienne includes the remains of a *fullonica* (fulling mill) from the second century CE. Another impressive site is the Musée départemental Arles antique.

By the third century, the Roman empire as a whole faced more difficulties, both from external attacks and as a result of internal problems, notably economic strain and disease. In response, in the late third and fourth centuries, the Romans fortified about 100 urban centres in Gaul with impressive stone walls. Those at Le Mans and Périgueux survive in part. There were also many lesser fortifications. Moreover, much of the elite moved from the cities to rural villas, where they enjoyed a degree of self-reliant protection and were in effect autonomous, not least from the urban authorities. This was the period in which major landowners imposed their patronage and power on free peasants, reducing them toward serfdom.

Meanwhile, religious movements spread across the empire. However, to an extent that was frequently subsequently under-played, there was no automatic turn to Christianity. Indeed, paganism continued for a couple of centuries, certainly in Brittany where the sixth century was the most active period of conversion. Mithraism, the Roman religion focused on the god Mithras, took hold and had centres at Bourg-Saint-Andéol, Saravi and Narbo, and Mithraic sites continue to be discovered, including at Angers and at Mariana, Corsica, in the 2010s. There were also Jewish communities, including in Lugdunum and Vienne. Yet Christianity was the most significant movement, replacing the Imperial Pantheon as the official religion. Episcopal centres, such as Saintes and Tours, gained importance accordingly. The oldest Christian building in France may be the Baptistery of Saint John in Poitiers. Early Christians risked martyrdom: Sainte Blandine, a slave, was martyred at Lyon in 177, while Saint Denis, the first Bishop of Lutetia, was allegedly beheaded around 250 on the hill of Montmartre before picking up his head and walking while preaching. According to tradition, he died at the site where a chapel was established by Sainte Geneviève in 475, and where the present Basilique Saint-Denis stands. The first king to be buried in the basilica was the Frankish Dagobert I, who died in 639. Saint Devota, the patron saint of Corsica and Monaco, was allegedly martyred at Mariana in 303. Christianity became an accepted religion in Gaul in 311 and, in the form of Catholicism, the only authorized religion in 392.

Religious division was a cause of strain; but far more difficulty was caused by the pressure from outside. In response to 'Barbarian' attacks from across the Rhine, the Romans made arrangements with particular groups of 'Barbarians', including some of the Franks, originally Germanic peoples. These groups provided troops to help the Romans, but this in effect led to a longer-term process of 'Barbarianization' in northern Gaul and large-scale attacks. Always unstable, the terms of this relationship changed in the fifth century, as the Roman governmental presence began to decline in northern and central Gaul. There was also a continued interaction of cooperation, however, as in 451 when Franks fought alongside Romans against Attila's Huns, defeating them at the battle of the Catalaunian Plains after the Huns had sacked Metz and Reims. In the end, Gaul did not so much succumb to the Germanic invaders of the fifth century as become transformed by them.

3. The Early Middle Ages

The landscape of post-Roman France was studded with evidence of conflict. This was not simply a matter of tribes and warlords. Indeed, the struggle between Good and Evil was dramatized in particular locations where the Archangel Michael was believed to have fought the Devil, as in the Meuse Valley near Sedan and at Mont Dol on the Breton coast. Michael, as a warrior figure who had overcome the Devil himself, was a particularly inspired choice to counter the warlike or vengeful pagan gods and to attract the fierce tribes who worshipped them. Belief in the real presence of evil resulted in dubbing features located in deep caves as 'gates of Hell', such as the hole at the bottom of the Fosse Dionne, a pool at Tonnerre.

Less dramatically, several 'Barbarian' tribes, under pressure from others further east, moved into Gaul from the late fourth century. Some passed through to conquests elsewhere, notably the Vandals en route to North Africa, and the Suevi en route to western Iberia. Others settled, among them the Franks, Burgundians, Alemanni and Visigoths. The Roman administrators of Gaul sought to placate the invaders, hiring them as soldiers and giving them land, as with the Visigoths in the south-west from the mid-410s and the Salian Franks in the region of Tournais. However, alongside a degree of admiration for Roman culture and of cultural, military and political assimilation, the 'Barbarians' retained and increasingly asserted their independence, forming a series of principalities, for example the Visigothic kingdom of Toulouse. As with other parts of the Roman empire, there is considerable debate about the extent of continuity or discontinuity after the end of Roman rule, and there was certainly not only much disruption but also major changes, for example with the impact on the economy of the marked fall in exports to Italy.

The Franks, whose name apparently meant 'free or fierce ones', became, in the fifth century, the dominant group across much of France, Belgium and Germany, terms used here to capture modern geographical locations and not expressing any political divisions of the period. The Franks were initially based in Belgium and Germany but, at Soissons in 486 under Clovis (r. 481–511), they defeated Syagrius, the ruler of the Roman-controlled area in what is now northern France. Clovis also drove the Visigoths from southern France in 507, winning victory at Campus Vogladensis (Vouillé) near Poitiers, and defeated the Alemanni in the east.

By converting to Christianity, Clovis won a degree of legitimation, gained the support of the Gallo-Roman aristocracy and the Church, and became the champion of Catholic orthodoxy against the Arian tendency. All this facilitated the bridging of Gallo-Roman and Frankish culture, and the ease of changing cultural identity – from Roman to 'Frank', the source of the name Francia, and later France. The Basilique Saint-Remi in Reims, named after the bishop who, probably in 496, baptized Clovis and his warriors, contains early Romanesque sections. Clovis established his residence at Paris, and as 'Barbarian' rulers elsewhere, notably the Ostrogoths in Italy, agreed to rule as a form of honorary consul on behalf of the Byzantine (Eastern Roman) emperor. This was important in cultivating a sense, then and later, of continuity between the Roman empire and the kingdom of France.

The defeat of the Visigoths in 507 was a major step in the move toward a France in which the south looked to the north, and not to a transmontane link with Italy or Spain (the Visigoths had looked to Spain as their centre of power was at Toulouse). This outcome was far from inevitable and deserves attention as part of the fundamental uncertainty of politics, namely that of an inherent unpredictability about the geography of the state in question. Clovis, who was reported to have killed Alaric II, the Visigoth king, in the battle, pressed on to capture Toulouse. As a result of the expansion of the Franks, the cities of the south-east, such as Arles, became of less consequence.

Like other 'Barbarian' rulers, Clovis consolidated his kingdom by murdering many of his relatives, yet jeopardized it by dividing his succession among his sons and grandsons. Clovis set up the Merovingian dynasty so that the leadership of the Franks was hereditary within the family, rather than elective, but the absence of primogeniture – through which the eldest male inherits everything – meant that his four sons partitioned his lands. This did not lead to stability and, instead, murder and feud fed division, a process encouraged by the absence of any firm conventions on marriage and succession. Rulers tended to leave sons by different partners; those sons, and their spouses, frequently sought – for their own ends – to reconstitute the unity of the Frankish kingdom.

Yet, alongside division, the Merovingians saw formidable expansion, including the conquest, in 534, of previously independent Burgundy, and the acquisition of Provence from the Italian-based Ostrogoths in 537. This was a parallel to the driving out of the Visigoths from the south-west. There was also expansion beyond the bounds of what would later be France, including imposing a protectorate over Turingia (in 531), the Alemanni (536) and the Bavarians (555), and controlling northern Italy, albeit only between 540 and 550. This expansion, which reflected the interest of the Franks in the lands to the east of their kingdom, looked toward the later drive of the kings of France to reach and even pass the

Rhine. In contrast, French expansionism was not to be directed towards Iberia or England.

Based in Soissons, Chlothar I, one of Clovis's sons, reunited the Frankish kingdom in 558. He ruled all of modern France, excluding Septimania (eastern Languedoc) and much of modern Brittany, and also most of modern Switzerland, the Rhineland and the Low Countries (Belgium and the Netherlands). In turn, Chlothar's death in 561 was followed by a partition between his four surviving sons, and fresh conflict. On a longstanding pattern of division, this partition led to pulls in different directions, with Austrasia in the north-east, Neustria in the north-west (capital: Paris) and Burgundy as the three key units. Aquitaine, meanwhile, was deprived of its south-eastern regions when Marseille was given to Neustria, and Aix and Avignon to Burgundy. This situation prefigured the later partition of Lotharingia, and, indeed, the short-lived and arbitrary character of medieval territorial divisions.

The Merovingians drew on a range of traditions, including Germanic, Roman and Christian ones, to provide a sense of identity and legitimacy. Roman and Christian traditions in particular, at least in theory, separated the rulers from the aristocrats by asserting that the dynasty had higher origins than the aristocrats, including the dukes who were the key administrative figures. The dynasty's distinguished origins were presented as fact, as in the *Decem Libri Historiarum* (Ten Books of History), better known as *Historia Francorum* (see pl. III), written by Gregory, Bishop of Tours (*c.* 538–594). This provided an account of the Creation, the origins of Christianity, the story of Saint Martin and the beginnings of Gregory's see of Tours.

Politics was a spoils system – and therefore a basis for dispute – in which kings, dukes, other aristocrats and clerics were all land-owners, and the payments, produce and services they received as a result kept the entire system going. This manorial system rested on the agricultural services provided by serfs and (free) peasants whose labour was gruelling and whose rewards were few. The wealth of the landowners was used to produce valuable objects that were prestige symbols, as can be seen in the treasures of Merovingian culture that are preserved in the impressive Musée d'archéologie nationale in Saint-Germain-en-Laye, Île-de-France. Church building was part of the same process, as was the accumulation of relics, the two linked in saints' cults that were designed to convey a form of white magic. Saints were believed to have an effect upon the place where their human remains were found, which helped to explain the successful cult of relics, not least as medicine was so poorly developed.

The Church was a key agency of authority, power, wealth and social mobility, and also provided continuity from the Roman period, not least through the ability of aristocratic families from that period to dominate the ranks of the bishops. This, indeed, was an aspect of the more general grounding of an aristocracy in state and Church, one that brought together the Franks and the Romans.

This aristocracy in practice shared power with the monarchs, a process encouraged by divisions among the Merovingian house. Monarchs and aristocrats manoeuvred for advantage, with murder a frequent means of politics, as well as marriage strategies that could help give power to particular women. There was also opposition between Austrasia and Burgundy on the one hand, each concerned to defend their distinctiveness, and Neustria, which defended the unity of the kingdom.

By the end of the seventh century, disunity within the Merovingian house was matched by growing independence on the part of aristocrats and, especially, the 'mayor of the palace' or leading minister. At the same time, existing social and cultural links among the Franks, and between them and their subjects, ensured that the Merovingian kingdom did not collapse, while annual meetings of ruler and aristocracy helped ensure continuity. Pepin of Herstal, mayor of the palace of Austrasia from 680, conquered Neustria and Burgundy in 687, making himself mayor of the palace of all three kingdoms and calling himself Duke and Prince of the Franks, before extending Frankish power in the Low Countries and Germany.

Pepin's death in 714 led to a civil war between his son Charles Martel, 'the Hammer', and his grandson by another son, which the former won, including defeating the Merovingian king, Chilperic. Charles Martel then turned on foreign foes, defeating the Saxons in 718, seizing West Frisia in 719, and suppressing Bavarian and Alemanni opposition in a series of campaigns from 720 to 730. In 732, he gained crucial prestige at Poitiers by defeating Islamic invaders who had moved up from North Africa by crushing the Visigoths in 711 and conquering Spain and Portugal. After this victory, Charles Martel reintegrated Burgundy into the kingdom and obtained the submission of the Duke of Aquitaine, before intervening in Provence and thus restoring French influence there. In 737, when the Merovingian king died, Charles Martel left the position vacant. He died in 741, having divided his territories between his adult sons.

In turn, Martel's son, Pepin III (Pepin the Short), who had Papal support, in 751 deposed Childeric III, the last Merovingian king, and founded the Carolingian dynasty. Childeric's long hair, a symbol of the Merovingian dynasty, was cut off, and he and his son were placed in monasteries. Pepin went on to overcome opposition in southern France, campaign in Germany, and intervene in Italy against the Lombards.

Charlemagne (r. 768–814 as king of the Franks), Pepin III's son, and a great military leader, proved far more successful than the Merovingians, rather as Napoleon for much of his reign was more successful than his predecessors, the Bourbons. For neither man were there limits between 'France' and 'Italy', and both also campaigned far into Germany. As with Napoleon, Charlemagne's empire was sustained by wealth from campaigning as well as by an imperial ideology; although, in Charlemagne's case, religion in the shape of spreading Christianity and his sacred status, first as king of the Franks and then as emperor, also played a significant role. Indeed, status for Charlemagne was in part a product of the link with Italy that he won. Charlemagne's court at Aix-la-Chapelle (Aachen), and his role from 800 as 'emperor of the Romans', ensured that he cannot comfortably be annexed to French history, although that has never stopped the attempt, in part because his policies had an impact in what subsequently became France. Later kings were to be given the Sword of Charlemagne at their coronation and to be crowned with what was termed the Crown of Charlemagne, which was probably made for his grandson Charles the Bald. Relatively little Carolingian architecture survives in France, but the barrel-vaulted crypt of Saint Germain in Auxerre, with its frescoes of Saint Stephen, and the church of Saint Peter and Saint Paul at Ottmarsheim in Alsace are examples.

When Charlemagne's empire was divided among his heirs, in 817 and 843, the western kingdom was more clearly the basis for France. The Treaty of Verdun (843) created kingdoms roughly coterminous with modern France (although not Brittany) and western Germany, and, in addition, a middle kingdom comprising, initially, modern northern Italy, the Low Countries and a swathe of territory in between. In turn, by the Meerssen agreement of 870, the middle kingdom north of the Alps was divided between the two others.

As so often in French history, stability proved precarious because of external threat and internal division. Great pressure arose from a new bout of 'Barbarian' invaders, notably the Vikings.

They captured Angers in 854 and 872–73 and Rouen in 885, and besieged Paris in 885–86.

A LEGACY OF THE VIKING forays into Europe is indelibly inked on the French map. Expansion from Scandinavia transformed the map as the Vikings swept down the seas and rivers of Europe in their longboats. The raiding parties were often successful but, after their failed siege of Chartres, the Vikings agreed to the Treaty of Saint-Clair-sur-Epte in 911. Through this, the Carolingian ruler Charles III made a deal with the Norse warlord Rollo and handed him the duchy of Normandy. The Viking settlers were known as the Northmen, and from this we get the Normans and Normandy.

Viking devastation focused on the wealthy abbeys such as Noirmoutier at the mouth of the Loire in 799 and Jumièges on the Seine in 841. As a defence against their advances along rivers, fortified bridges were used, certainly at Pont-de-l'Arche on the Seine from 862, and probably at Les Ponts-de-Cé on the Loire in 873.

The Arab presence in Provence proved much more limited, both geographically and chronologically. Nevertheless, from their fortress at Fraxinetum (La Garde-Freinet) in 890 to 972, the Arabs, profiting from the divisions in Provençal society, raided southern France, especially the Rhône Valley. The kidnapping in 972 of the Fourth Abbot of Cluny, however, proved an action too far and led to a successful focus by the local nobility on driving the Arabs from Fraxinetum.

Meanwhile, provincial governors became more powerful as the monarchy weakened and its assets increasingly passed into the hands of aristocrats. When the last Carolingian, the childless Louis V, died young while hunting in 987, Hugues Capet was elected successor by an assembly of nobles, rather as Harold of Wessex was elected in England in 1066 after the death of the childless Edward 'the Confessor'. Capet had pedigree as he was a grandson of Robert I (r. 922–923) and, as duke of the Franks, the first noble of the kingdom. He was elected against the claim to the Crown of the legitimate Carolingian, Charles of Lorraine, because, unlike the latter, Capet was a French noble with French, and not German, as his native tongue. Thus, the national principle took precedence over the dynastic, as in the early fourteenth century with the preference for Philip VI, the first of the Valois dynasty, over Edward III of England.

THE BAYEUX TAPESTRY is one of the great historical artefacts of the medieval period and provides an unparalleled visual reference for historians. Despite its name, it is technically not a tapestry (it is an embroidery) and almost certainly not from Bayeux (it is now believed to have been made in Canterbury, England). The 70-metre (231-foot) cloth is an artistic treasure. It tells the story, in great and gory detail, of the Norman invasion of England in 1066 by William, Duke of Normandy, better known now as 'the Conqueror', against a backdrop of political turmoil in Europe. Believed to have been made within a few years of the invasion, it culminates in a bloody recreation of the Battle of Hastings at which Harold Godwinson, then king of England, is shown being killed by an arrow through the eye. The survival of the tapestry is one of its greatest feats having been very nearly cut up during the French Revolution, removed to Paris by Napoleon and taken once more by the Nazis during their occupation of France. In 2018 President Emmanuel Macron, against a backdrop of political turmoil in Europe, surprised many by promising that the tapestry would go on loan to the UK, the first time it will have left France.

Hugues Capet benefited in particular from the support of the Bishop of Laon and the Archbishop of Reims, the Church being a key force for cohesion throughout medieval France. This was seen in the respect paid to national saints, notably Martin and Denis, and in the support to the Capetian kings usually offered by the bishops of northern France. Anointed and crowned at Reims, Capet had a position akin to that of the earlier mayors of the palace, but this position was held in a state that lacked the power, wealth and prominence of the Carolingians at their height.

The comparison with Harold of Wessex, whose father, Earl Godwine, had held a position at court similar to a mayor of the palace, is instructive as it underlines the role of contingencies. The authority and power of the monarch was far greater in England than in France, but that, if anything, made England more of a target. Thus, the attack by Harald Hardrada, king of Norway, in 1066 was part of the pattern of Viking assaults on England. So too, to a degree, was that by William of Normandy. In contrast, despite the possibility of advancing up the Loire, Capetian France was less attractive a target, as well as being far less accessible for the Norwegians and Danes. Capetian France thereby benefited from the buffers offered by the surrounding autonomous territories, such as Normandy, but they provided only partial protection. The German-based emperors, notably from the Ottonian, Salian and Hohenstaufen dynasties, were to campaign repeatedly into Italy. In comparative terms, France was just as accessible to them, and notably so north-eastern France, including Paris, but France did not provide the wealth, prestige or power offered by campaigning into Italy. A very different comparison for the early Capetians is offered by the Popes who, alongside their far-flung pretensions, in practice were restricted in their power largely to a part of Italy. Yet, as in that case, the seedbed of later strength was already present.

Meanwhile, France was developing economically, not least with the land under cultivation increasing thanks to the clearance of woodland, as the population rose in a gradual recovery from the late sixth century onwards, and there was also a foundation of new settlements, which is reflected in placenames to this day, as with Neufchâteau (New Castle) and Châteauneuf-du-Pape (Pope's New Castle). Both continuing a longstanding process and reversing the decline of agrarian activity seen after the end of the Roman period, France became a more intensively worked landscape, although there were still extensive areas of woodland. Moreover, the low efficiency of agriculture meant that large numbers had to work the soil in order to provide what was only a modest surplus to feed others, notably nobles, clerics and townspeople.

This agrarian-based pyramidical society remained dominant until the socio-political changes of the French Revolution, and, separately, the socio-economic ones that began in the nineteenth century. A society of three orders was offered by Bishop Adalbéron of Laon, in his *Poème au roi Robert* (1027–30): at the top were the *oratores* and the *bellatores*, the clergy and the nobility, and at the base of the social pyramid, the *laborates*, the labourers. Economic intensification was seen from the late sixth century in urbanization and in the monetarization of life. Thus, the sceatta (a small silver coin), in circulation in northern France, the Low Countries and eastern England, in *c.* 680–740 ran into many millions. Particularly from the late seventh century, the so-called Dark Ages, therefore, were also a period of economic recovery and social development.

The shaping of what becomes modern France continued to be complex. Charlemagne's restructuring and strengthening of the system of the Marches – frontiers controlled by counts – defined his kingdom of France more narrowly than the 'hexagon' – the rough shape of modern France. In turn, these territories became autonomous.

4. Medieval France

A long string of famous cathedrals reveals the glories of medieval France. Chartres (see pl. VII), built from 1194 to 1260, is the most famous, but I prefer Bourges with the rich colours of its thirteenth-century stained glass, and Laon on its prominent site over the flatlands of Champagne. The castles from the period reveal the disunity of the medieval centuries but, amidst this disunity, cathedrals and monasteries testify to the Christian culture that was such a powerful source of identity in France.

Under its Capetian rulers, France embodied a classic form of the kind of hierarchical society that is often referred to as feudal, a system of political control and social organization that focused on a personal relationship between lord and vassal. Land was held accordingly and military service provided in return, the key element being by knights, who in their own person provided heavy cavalry and, as seigneurs or lords of the manor, mustered and organized the rank-and-file of the country. The feudal system led to a fragmented politics in which the local aristocracy wielded much of the power and, as a result, by the end of the tenth century the effective power of the king's writ was essentially confined to the Île-de-France, the area around Paris stretching south to the Loire.

Elsewhere, the counties and their courts ceased to be public institutions, and local official posts were absorbed into the patronage systems of the major aristocrats. Counts, such as Foulque Nerra (Fulk III the Black) of Anjou (r. 987–1040), who conquered

Touraine after a long struggle with Eudes II, Count of Blois, wielded considerable governmental powers, as did Baudoin V, Count of Flanders (r. 1035–1067) and Théobald III, Count of Blois (r. 1037–1089). They minted coins, raised troops and built castles, the last a powerful expression of autonomy. Indeed, Foulque Nerra reputedly built a hundred castles, which was not surprising given the number of his wars. Castles, often private fortified residences, were usually associated with the decline of public order and the privatization of power and, from the end of the tenth century, wooden ones were rebuilt in stone. These remain a mighty legacy, as seen with Montsoreau on the Loire, which was built by Count Odo I of Blois in 990. There was frequent conflict and militarily and politically incompetent and unsuccessful rulers did not survive, for example Geoffrey III of Anjou (r. 1060–1068), who was imprisoned and replaced by his brother, who became Foulque IV and proved an opponent of Normandy. Rulers also built monasteries, both to express devotion and to consolidate their control over territory and people.

The counts did not seek to replace the king as they scarcely needed to do so, for some, such as the Count of Toulouse and the Count of Champagne, were themselves as powerful as the king. Furthermore, Aquitaine and Toulouse, both south of the Loire, were sufficiently distant from Paris to be little concerned about its Capetian rulers. North of the Loire, however, rivalry between the powerful local feudatories and the Crown was more important. The union of Blois and Champagne for some time produced a powerful ruler both to the east and west of the Île-de-France. The dukes of Normandy, meanwhile, competed with the Capetians, in particular for control of the Vexin to the north-west of Paris, but also more generally. Following a different path, Brittany had been largely brought under control by Charlemagne in 799, but within three years of his death in 814, the Bretons were already in revolt against the Franks. Frankish suzerainty (feudal lordship) was overthrown in 843 and, after a series of victories, Brittany became a kingdom from 851 to 952.

The idea of a powerful French monarchy was kept alive by the Church, but there was little basis to it in the eleventh century. Indeed, Robert II (r. 996–1031), Henry I (r. 1031–1060) and Philip I (r. 1060–1108) achieved most by hanging on, and despite Robert temporarily holding Burgundy, they did not make gains comparable to Guillaume (William) I, Duke of Normandy, who survived attacks by Henry in 1054 and 1058, and conquered England in 1066, sailing from Saint-Valéry-sur-Somme where an impressive citadel survives. One bishop remarked to Robert, 'You may be a king among serfs, but you are a serf among kings.' In the twelfth century, Louis VI (r. 1108–1137) and Louis VII (r. 1137–1180) struggled to expand Capetian power, but with limited success. Louis VI backed opposition to Henry I of England in Normandy, but unsuccessfully so.

A major setback occurred in 1152 when Louis VII allowed his divorced wife, Eleanor of Aquitaine (whom he had married in 1137), to marry Henry's grandson, Henry, Duke of Normandy and Count of Anjou, thereby losing effective control of a large portion of southern France. Combined with the Norman inheritance that Henry had won, this made Henry – Henry II of England (r. 1154–1189) – the most powerful ruler in France, and far more so than his suzerain for those French territories, Louis. Henry also used this power to intervene in succession disputes, by this means bringing the dukes of Brittany within his influence from 1158 along with more of southern France from 1159. Thus, France's destiny appeared nearly as much set by Henry as Louis VI 'the Fat'. Under Henry, much of France was part of his greater European polity that included England and was expanding into Wales and Ireland, and he was also putting pressure on

Scotland. Indeed, far from being identified with England, Henry, who died at Chinon, his estranged wife Eleanor and son Richard the Lionheart (Richard I, r. 1189–1199), who died fighting in France, were entombed in the peaceful Abbaye de Fontevraud in Anjou. In order to increase the prestige of the dynasty among its subjects and to rebuild royal power, Henry sought to suppress private wars in the royal domain and to support the free peasantry so as to keep them on the land.

The Capetians offered a different legacy to the Norman and Angevin (i.e. of Anjou) kings of England. Ancestors and epic leaders from the past appeared in the tomb effigies in the choirs of the basilicas of Saint-Denis (Paris) and Saint-Remi (Reims). In England, the Norman and Angevin kings were representatives of a type of monarchy in which the king was, first and foremost, 'lord', and then administrator of a mass of wealth and power; rather than, like the Capetians, kings who derived their power from atavistic roots in tribe and nation, and from laying an emphasis on the holiness of the king's person. The sacrality of the Capetian kings was emphasized by their anointment with the holy oil reputedly brought down from Heaven by a dove for the anointing of Clovis and which thereafter miraculously reproduced itself. This myth invested the Capetian kings with immense mystique, a mystique with which the English kings, who were short of origin myths, could not compete.

French culture was highly influential in international developments, notably the replacement of the Romanesque architectural style by the Gothic, a style born there, which very much became the visual language of medieval France. As is clearly seen with the basilica of Saint-Denis, in Paris's northern suburbs, Gothic buildings, with their pointed windows and their verticality, were much lighter than those of the Romanesque. The length of time taken to build many church buildings ensures that the change in style can be understood in particular sites, for example the cloister of the cathedral at Elne, in Roussillon. The rebuilding of Sens cathedral began in the 1130s in traditional Romanesque style but, all of a sudden, the old scheme was abandoned and replaced with the revolutionary new style of Saint-Denis. Prominent Gothic examples worthy of note include not only the famous cathedrals, one of the largest and highest being Amiens, built in 1220–69, but also Avignon, with its Papal palace and the remains of its bridge. The construction of Notre-Dame in Paris, begun in 1163 and completed in 1345 (although largely finished by 1260), made much use of the rib vault and the flying buttress, as well as having large windows.

France also took a lead in monasticism, not least through the major role taken up by the Benedictine order of Cluny, founded in 910, which was one of the largest churches in Christendom. More centrally, the Cistercian order was founded in 1098 at the village of Citeaux near Dijon as a more observant alternative to following the rule of Saint Benedict. The Cistercians became particularly important in France, with the first daughter house at La Ferté (1113) and the influence of Bernard of Clairvaux (Saint Bernard) being significant. Despite massive destruction at the time of the French Revolution, there are remains – notably the abbeys of Flaran and Fontenay, and the church at Pontigny, the monks of which developed Chablis wine – on the pattern of many other monasteries.

As an aspect of the role of the Church, intellectual development owed much to the encouragement of clerics. Chartres became a major centre in the early eleventh century, and scholars at the school included Bernard of Chartres, Thierry of Chartres and Guillaume of Conches, with the first half of the twelfth century proving an apogee before activity was refocused on the new University of Paris, a major centre of learning. The achievements of the twelfth-century Renaissance owed much to France. Philosophy was applied to theology and there was an interest in Classical Greek works. The Chartres thinkers developed ideas of knowability linked to scientific empiricism, i.e. knowledge was to be based in proven fact rather than purely belief, and they were ready to accept contingent and changing results in place of clear-cut certainty. The belief that doubt would be clarified by information deployed by a God-given human intellect was crucial in the assertion of this new rationalism. Theory had to accommodate fact, which offered a workable space and method for what can be seen as science, as with the work, at Paris in the fourteenth century, of Nicole Oresme, who plotted the speed of an object against time. However, in the thirteenth century, the University of Paris became a focus for scholasticism, a systematic rationalism that did not welcome doubt.

Meanwhile, the decisive growth of the French royal domain, that part of the kingdom under the direct control of the king, rather than under powerful feudal vassals, occurred later, under the determined Philip Augustus (r. 1180–1223) who had been an opponent of Henry II and rival of Richard I in the leadership of the Third Crusade. The first to style himself king of France as opposed to of the Franks, Philip's drive and military and political success led to King John of England (r. 1199–1216) losing Anjou and Normandy in 1203–5. The successful French siege of Chinon in 1204–5 was crucial to the fate of Anjou and Touraine. Finally, exploiting the crisis of John's last years, and the weakness of his son Henry III's minority, Philip's son, Louis, later Louis VIII (r. 1223–1226), claimed the English throne, only for his invasion of England to be defeated in 1217. Nevertheless, it was now plausible for the French to attack England, or to support its rivals within the British Isles, beginning a situation of threat that ended only in the nineteenth century.

Among Philip's other achievements were a strengthening of the government and an attempt to develop links with the towns, so that they looked to the Crown and not to the nobility, which helped to check the power of the latter. Philip enhanced Paris by constructing a major wall and the beginnings of the Louvre, as a fort; granting a charter to the university in 1200; and developing Les Halles, a major market begun in 1135 by Louis VI.

The scale of France, however, was such that a largely different narrative can be offered for the situation in the south, although there was an important overlap, notably in the role of the king. The crusade in this region against the Cathar (Albigensian) heresy led eventually to an increase in royal power but, again, chance factors played a key role. Pope Innocent III, also an opponent of John of England at this juncture, proclaimed a crusade in 1209 and the ambitious Simon de Montfort, accordingly, overran much of Languedoc, Carcassonne falling after a short siege. Now a much visited site, the Cité there is in fact largely the product of a somewhat heavy-handed mid-nineteenth-century restoration. The crusaders slaughtered thousands, notably at Béziers.

In 1213, Peter II of Aragon intervened in the conflict. An orthodox Catholic, he was concerned about de Montfort's rising power, and backed Count Raymond VI of Toulouse, with whom de Montfort was at war. Their united forces, nevertheless, were defeated at Muret in 1213, Peter was killed, and the crusaders occupied Toulouse. But warfare and politics remained uncertain. The war came to an end in 1224, only to be renewed in 1225, ending in 1229 when Raymond VII of Toulouse signed the Treaty of Paris. His daughter Joan was obliged to marry Alphonse de Poitiers, a younger son of Louis VIII, and, when Raymond died in 1249, Alphonse became count of Toulouse. In turn, when he died in 1271, the county was annexed to France. Remote Montségur held out until 1244, when the Cathars who refused to recant were burnt: the windy site is a chilling one.

The warfare might appear confusing, but, as so often in France's history, there were key results. Expeditions in 1219 and 1226 by Louis, first as prince and then as Louis VIII, helped to strengthen royal influence in the region, just as those by Louis XIII and Louis XIV to southern France were to do in the seventeenth century. Avignon was successfully besieged in 1226 when it opposed the passage of the royal army. Moreover, the defeat of Aragon decisively weakened a long-lasting link between southern France and Catalonia. This was part of a more lasting process, looking back to Frankish success against the Visigoths in the sixth century, in which southern France was configured northwards, rather than remaining separate or looking to Catalonia (although, for a while, southern France looked across the western Mediterranean toward North Africa and then Italy as part of the warlike plans of Louis IX and Charles of Anjou). Moreover, the suppression of religious heterodoxy had an impact, and there was to be no comparable movement in medieval France, while the crusade against the Albigensians was employed as an example in the late sixteenth century by Catholics arguing the case against religious pluralism. Thus the Cathars unwittingly laid the groundwork for a more cohesive France in terms of both state and Church.

In the thirteenth century, the French continued to make gains. In 1224, war with England resumed, and Louis VIII successfully invaded Poitou and northern Aquitaine, although Bordeaux and Gascony remained faithful to Henry III, in part because of their commercial links with England, notably wine exports. By the Treaty of Paris (1259), Henry renounced his rights to Normandy, Anjou and Poitou. This was a recognition of his own failure and that of his father. It also began over a half-century in which the English presence in France was considered restricted, which helped consolidate French control over much of the country where it had previously been limited. The failure by the Norman and

Angevin kings to create a permanent, stable, trans-Channel identity and polity was to interact with the development of national consciousness in England and France.

Twelfth- and thirteenth-century warfare has left its mark today in terms of fortified sites, the most impressive being Château Gaillard (Strong Castle), situated in a raised position on the banks of the River Seine. Built by Richard I of England in 1196–98, it was captured from his brother John by the forces of Philip Augustus in 1204. Magnificently strong castles such as this were helpless if separated from their broader logistical support system. Château Gaillard was isolated by the besieging force, which blocked the Seine and prevented a relief force from reaching the castle. A relief force advancing by land was also driven off, and the castle eventually starved into surrender. Its seizure left Normandy vulnerable to rapid conquest, Rouen falling soon after. The castle was partly destroyed by Henry IV of France in 1603 in the aftermath of the Wars of Religion. Furthermore, in 1228–38, the French built a still-impressive castle at Angers that was designed to consolidate their position in Anjou.

Very differently, between 300 and 500 walled towns known as *bastides* were built in the south-west in the thirteenth century, to a common design. Many extant examples are largely unchanged. The most active founders of *bastides* were Alphonse de Poitiers, Count of Toulouse (r. 1249–1271), who built fifty-seven, and Edward I of England (r. 1272–1307), Duke of Aquitaine, who sought by this means to consolidate his hold on the northern borders of his duchy. Edward's *bastides* include well-preserved Monpazier.

The cultural context of war was not constant, as national identity was developing. Writing in the vernacular became common from the mid-thirteenth century, with texts such as the *Histoire Ancienne* and the *Grandes Chroniques de France*. The latter, which appeared in considerable quantities, included translations of Latin chronicles and was associated with Saint Denis, and was a sort of an exemplary official history of the monarchy. The rise of lay literacy was important to the changing political and cultural context.

National identity, however, could have unattractive manifestations, as when Louis VIII overturned his father's willingness to allow royal officials to register debts owed to Jews. Over this and other issues, Louis found himself opposed by Thibaut IV, Count of Champagne. It is easy to forget such rivalries in concentrating on that with the Angevins and, later, the Burgundians, but there was a serious tension with much of the nobility. In 1230–31, Pierre Count of Brittany rebelled, with English encouragement; his rebellion was contained, but not overcome, whereas, in 1242, an English-backed rebellion in Poitou was crushed. There was also the tension created by the granting of apanages – estates and titles – to the younger sons of the king. This left Artois, Poitou, Auvergne, Anjou and Maine to sons of Louis VIII, although only one of the younger sons lived to adulthood.

Louis IX (r. 1226–1270) was to distinguish himself by his support for the Church. In 1240–42, in a 'trial' in Paris, rabbis were obliged to deny charges that the Talmud insulted Christianity and, in 1242, large numbers of the book were burned in Paris. Two years later, in response to serious ill health, Louis promised to go on crusade if he survived. With Papal support for Louis, the Church in France provided funds, for the cost of the crusade was formidable, and further funds were raised by a purge of the allegedly corrupt. Louis developed Aigues-Mortes as an embarkation port for the crusade. Leaving France in 1248, he invaded Egypt in 1249, only to be heavily defeated in 1250 at al-Mansura. Louis was captured, but his mother, Blanche of Castile, ran the country in his absence until 1252.

Louis did not return until 1254. The Christian theme was then pushed anew, with probity in government presented accordingly, as well as legislation against corruption, blasphemy and usury, and pressure on Jews to convert. Louis's reform programme was conceived as a response to his failure on crusade: he felt that he had to atone for what he thought were his sins by offering better justice and better government to his subjects. Hospitals were founded for the poor, and charity encouraged. Ambition abroad led to support for the extensive Italian and Balkan ambitions of Louis's brother Charles of Anjou, and contributed to another crusade, mounted against Tunis in 1270, on which Louis died of disease. Charles of Anjou became count of Provence by marriage and forced Marseille to acknowledge his suzerainty. However, the wider Angevin empire he created proved ephemeral, notably due to opposition from Aragon. This empire was an instance of French ambition in the Mediterranean, which was to prove a longstanding theme, one that survives in the control over Corsica.

Louis's successor, Philip III (r. 1270–1285), succeeded his father in command of the crusade and, despite ill health, returned safely. Seeking to maintain Louis's legacy, pressing for his canonization and continuing measures against the Jews, Philip also sustained the royal presence in the south. He encountered significant resistance but, in 1271, successfully offered Lyon protection against local barons. His intervention in Spanish politics proved less successful, with war with Castile in 1276 proving indecisive and the invasion of Aragon in 1285 a serious failure. Philip died on the retreat, leaving the throne to his son, who became Philip IV the Fair (r. 1285–1314). Peace followed in 1290.

Edward I of England was an opponent of Philip IV. Each talented and energetic, they fought in 1294–1303, and Philip therefore backed opposition to Edward in Scotland. Both rulers found it difficult to fund their expensive war, and Philip also faced opposition in Flanders, where a French army was heavily defeated at Courtrai in 1302, a major event in France's longstanding effort to dominate the region.

In a key display of power, Philip showed great brutality in his suppression of the Templar Order in 1307–14, which culminated with the burning of many Templars at the stake in Paris on trumped-up charges of idolatry, a campaign that enabled him to wipe out his debts to the order. The attack on an international religious order prefigured that on the Jesuits in the late eighteenth century.

The position of strength was swiftly followed by the end of the dynasty, a major instance of the unpredictability of history. Philip was succeeded by his son Louis X (r. 1314–1316), but the latter's early death left a contested succession, with his brother Philip V (r. 1316–1322) refuting the claims of Louis's daughter Joan. Philip's successor, Charles IV (r. 1322–1328), the last of the direct line of the Capetian dynasty, defeated his brother-in-law, Edward II of England, in 1324 in the War of Sardos, but died without children.

The situation deteriorated far further for France under Edward I's grandson, Edward III (r. 1327–1377), who broadened his opposition to Philip VI (r. 1328–1350), the paternal first cousin of Charles IV and the first monarch of the Valois dynasty, by claiming the French throne in 1337, thus beginning the Hundred Years War (1337–1453). Edward's mother, Isabella, was the daughter of Philip IV, and Edward, therefore, claimed the succession via the female line, a means rejected by the Valois who, thanks to the exclusion of female inheritance by means of the Salic Law, inherited the throne through the male.

In the beginning of the Hundred Years War, Edward III exploited disputes in Flanders and Brittany, in both of which the authority of the French Crown was limited. Indeed, the war was in part a French civil war, superficially brought about by the change of dynasty, but involving, at its heart, a rebellion by the French provincial elites against the centralizing policies of the monarchy. The fortunes of war were mixed, but the use of longbowmen helped the English win major victories against larger forces at Crécy (1346) and Poitiers (1356). These victories led to the Peace of Brétigny (1360), in which Edward promised to renounce his claim to the French throne, to Normandy and to Anjou, but was recognized, in return, as duke of the whole of Aquitaine as well as ruler of Calais, which had been captured in 1347. John II of France (r. 1350–1364) promised to renounce his claim to sovereignty over Edward's continental dominions, so that Edward would hold what he had in full sovereignty; but the treaty was never ratified. Moreover, in the face of French pressure, Edward's acquisitions proved difficult to maintain and, by the Truce of Bruges (1375), Edward held little more than Calais, Bordeaux and Bayonne.

Meanwhile, France expanded its power in the Rhône Valley, and in 1349 purchased Dauphiné, a major gain to the east of the river. Further north, however, the duchy of Burgundy, in theory a French fief, became more independent and powerful under Philip the Bold (r. 1363–1404), the youngest son of John II. John's willingness to give appanages to his younger sons, Philip the Bold, Louis, Duke of Anjou and John, Duke of Berry, threatened the cohesion of the state. The process also benefited the sons of John's successor, Charles V (r. 1364–1380): his younger son, Louis, became Duke of Orléans in 1392. During this time, the overall situation was one of flux. Royal authority was far weaker in practice than in theory, and a geographical notion of nationhood was subject to the very changeable power politics of the period.

A very different form of instability to that of dynastic and aristocratic rivalry, but one that drew on it, was a constitutional reform advanced in 1356–58 by Étienne Marcel, the provost of the merchants of Paris, and therefore the leader of the Third Estate. This was the mercantile class in the Estates-General, France's version of a parliament. (The other two – higher – estates or orders of the realm in the Estates-General were the clergy and the nobility.) Marcel sought to bring in public control of the government, only for this programme to collapse. In part, the failure was due to the chaos of an anti-noble peasant rising, the *Jacquerie*, north of Paris in 1358; but it was also due to the opposition of the nobility and, increasingly, of the bourgeoisie to the violence associated with Marcel. He was assassinated and is commemorated by a statue in Paris next to the Hôtel de Ville.

Economic difficulties, meanwhile, were of growing significance. In 1300, the population was seventeen million, making France the most populous kingdom in western Europe, but the growth of population placed intense pressure on the land. The strains upon rural and urban society stemming from the Black Death plague epidemic of the late 1340s, which hit France hard, exacerbated social divisions and the *Jacquerie* reflected the pressures on the rural economy and the desperation caused. The suppression of the *Jacquerie* by noble forces was particularly brutal, with many thousands of peasants slaughtered: the noble cavalry enjoyed a military advantage. There was another revolt in 1382, that of the *Harelle* at Rouen, a tax revolt.

The economy of the period can be seen in the illustrations from the *Très Riches Heures du Duc de Berry*, a book of hours (a collection of religious texts) created between 1412 and 1416 that is preserved at Chantilly. They depict the activities of July, including sheep shearing and the harvesting of wheat, which are both labour-intensive and, therefore, encourage landlords to maintain control over the peasantry. Longstanding patterns of agricultural activity continued, as they still do today, albeit with the major changes subsequent to mechanization. Thus the Fête de la transhumance in Saint-Rémy-de-Provence provides an annual celebration of the age-old dispatch in the late spring of animals from the lowlands to high grazing.

The French Crown under Charles VI (r. 1380–1422) failed to reassert royal authority convincingly in the late fourteenth century, and this issue was taken further when Charles, from 1392, was hit by serious problems of mental health. The initiative in the Hundred Years War, however, was not regained by the English until Henry V invaded in 1415, employing cannon as a key force-enabler in capturing well-fortified Harfleur. Relying on his longbowmen, he went on to defeat the French at Agincourt, a battle that can be followed at the Centre Historique Médiéval d'Azincourt, as well as on the battlefield. On his second expedition in 1417, Henry conquered much of Normandy, storming Caen after its walls were breached.

Henry V was greatly helped by an alliance with the Duke of Burgundy, the bitter rival of the Orléanists. Indeed, throughout the Hundred Years War, the successes of the King of England owed much to French allies, with the conflict in part an international dimension to a series of French civil wars. Alongside civil war, there was an internationalization in terms of the drawing into the conflict of the Flemish cities as allies of England, and of Scotland and Castile as allies of France. Moreover, by 1400, the political alignments in Europe largely mirrored those in the Church in the (Papal) Great Schism (1378–1417). Civil war, however, was not how the Hundred Years War was to be remembered in France. As a reminder of different cross-currents of influence and power, magic, divination and astrology played a major role in the courts of both John the Fearless and Philip the Good of Burgundy.

Henry V's victories led in 1420 to marriage, in the Church of Saint Jean au Marché in Troyes, to Catherine, daughter of Charles VI. By the Treaty of Troyes, he was recognized as Charles's heir and as regent during his life. The French Dauphin, later Charles VII (r. 1422–1461), continued to resist, and Henry, whose area of control did not extend south of the Loire Valley, died in 1422, probably of dysentery, while on campaign near Paris. His baby son, Henry VI, was proclaimed king of France when Charles VI died in the same year. The English strove to maintain Henry V's impetus and had success until 1429, not least with a major, though hard-fought, victory at Verneuil in 1424, and there appeared to be no reason why Henry V's success should not be consolidated in the person of Henry VI, a grandson of Charles VI. Long called the 'Roi de Bourges', Charles VII, however, was energized by the charismatic and young Joan of Arc (1412–1431), who was from a peasant family at Domrémy and who claimed to have received visions from saints instructing her to help Charles (see pl. IV). In 1429, she accompanied an army that broke the English siege at Orléans: a lack of English manpower ensured that the siege-works were incomplete. That year, Charles was crowned at Reims.

Joan was captured by the Burgundians, handed over to the English, tried for heresy and burned to death in the marketplace in Rouen in 1431; but the resistance had charged anew and that change was sustained. In 1435, crucially, the Burgundians abandoned Henry VI. Paris was regained in 1436 and the English, divided at home, were outmanoeuvred politically and militarily, although, in part, this was a matter of relative success. Thus, Charles VII had to face rebellious magnates in 1437 and, even more, the *Praguerie* revolt of 1440, named after the tendency to revolt of the Hussites of the modern Czech Republic. In turn, the English government sought a compromise with France. Indeed, Henry VI married Margaret of Anjou in 1445 and ceded Maine to Charles, but, unpopular in itself in England, this move did not settle the conflict.

In 1445, benefiting from his strengthening of royal control over taxation, Charles established *compagnies d'ordonnance*, a standing-army system consisting of heavy cavalry units under leading nobles.

Each company wore the livery of the captain and he selected those appointed and frequently had to rely on his own personal credit to fund them. There was a reluctance, however, to arm the peasantry. In 1449–51, Normandy and Gascony, England's remaining possessions other than Calais, fell swiftly to Charles's superior army, not least his artillery. Intimidation was a key tool, in particular because English garrisons were small and the chances of relief slim. The French would negotiate the inhabitants' surrender, which would take effect if there was no relief, usually within two weeks. If surrendering, the garrison could leave with its belongings, promising not to fight for two or three months. If not, then the garrison would forfeit their lives once the fort was taken. The Bureau brothers, the commanders of the French cannon, displayed their skill at the siege of Cherbourg in 1450 with the cannon placed on the sands so that they could cover the sea-facing wall of the fortress. The cannon could be left in place when the tide came in, ready for reuse when the tide receded. In 1453, an English riposte in Gascony was crushed at Castillon, with the French using cannon successfully in defence.

The English were left holding only Calais and the Channel Islands, and the French were to recapture the first in 1558. The Valois kings in the mid-fifteenth century appeared the most powerful rulers in western Europe, with national identity built up in part by the long war. With the Luxembourg dynasty facing continual opposition from the Hussites in Bohemia, and both England and Castile affected by civil conflict, Charles could now seek to consolidate royal authority and to expand French power.

Charles and, even more, his son and successor, Louis XI (r. 1461–1483), faced key problems seen by their predecessors, notably the imposition on the major aristocrats, especially the dukes of Burgundy, of recognition of the power of the Crown, and the attempt to incorporate Flanders into the kingdom. The latter failed, although Picardy was gained, as, for a while, was Artois. The relative success of the monarchs launched France as what was later termed one of the New Monarchies: these were assertive states that possessed a greater degree of central authority than a monarchy with a more feudal character. Sir John Fortescue, in the 1470s, in his *Governance of England: otherwise called The Difference between an Absolute and a Limited Monarchy*, 'singled out the quality of collegiality of crown and subjects as the essence of the English political system, something that distinguished it from France'. The former he described as a *dominium politicum et regale* (political and regal kingdom), the latter as *dominium regale*. Whereas, in England, government required the cooperation of a free political society, in France, there were no effective institutional checks, such as parliamentary assent to legislation and taxation.

Nevertheless, there were also effective bridles to royal power. The functional problems of government were crucial: France was far larger than England, and there were major limitations in internal communications. The sheer physical limitations of distance, resources and manpower, and the governmental obstacles of local interests and a shortage of information, were considerable. Moreover, Crown policy was constrained by cadres of officials who, in practice, served the interests of aristocratic factions, and its authority by conventions of good kingship and government. Yet, the monarchy was the core around which France was successfully rebuilt in the later stages of the Hundred Years War, and it was understood in that light.

For France, this success, and thus authority, arose in large part not only from crushing English power on the Continent, but also from overthrowing that of Burgundy, which had expanded greatly under Philip the Bold (r. 1363–1404) and Philip the Good (r. 1419–1467), including gaining Artois and Picardy. Charles the Bold (r. 1467–1477) added Alsace and became involved in Lorraine.

Buoyed up by the commercial growth of the Low Countries, which it had also acquired, Burgundy was a threat to France, its forces besieging Paris in 1465. On top of that, Louis XI confronted rebellious barons, notably in the war against the League of the Public Weal (1465–69), deploying cannon accordingly with success. He also faced an English invasion under Edward IV in 1475: Edward, a Yorkist, was linked to the Burgundians, whereas Louis supported the rival Lancastrians. His son, Charles VIII (r. 1483–1498), was to back Henry Tudor's successful overthrow of Richard III in 1485 with troops and equipment.

The mid to late 1470s saw a more serious crisis for France than the last stages of the Hundred Years War, but the English did not persist, while the Burgundian army was totally defeated by the Swiss at Nancy in 1477, and Charles the Bold killed. This was a turning point in French history. The Burgundian inheritance was then partitioned between Louis XI, whose gains included Picardy and Burgundy, and the Habsburgs, who established themselves in the Low Countries. France retained most of Louis's gains, a major geopolitical change: alongside the role of force, the winning over of a wide range of local notables was crucial to this power. Their continued local power was complemented by the extension of the royal affinity into the region. Memorials from the period include, in Beauvais, the statue of Jeanne Hachette, a local version of Joan of Arc who helped in the defence of the city against Charles the Bold in 1472.

Louis XI also gained suzerainty over Provence in 1481 after the death of the last count, although the authority of the Crown there was a matter of being count of Provence as well as king. The spread of the royal domain was pressed further forward when Charles VIII took control of the independent duchy of Brittany. A crushing victory over the Bretons at Saint-Aubin-du-Cormier in 1488 was followed by Francis II of Brittany accepting harsh terms. Dynastic marriages were used to cement Brittany within France. Francis's daughter and successor, Anne, married Charles in 1491 and, after the childless Charles's death, married Louis XII (who had divorced his first wife) in 1499; her daughter, Claude, married the future Francis I in 1514 and ceded her husband the duchy in 1532.

France was now both successful and coherent territorially to an extent that would have seemed fantastic a century earlier.

5. Renaissance France, 1494–1598

From triumph to civil war: from a French army entering Naples in 1495, to Henry III being forced out of rebellious Paris in 1588, the long sixteenth century was a switchback ride of uncertainty. The most vivid episode, the massacre of French Protestants on Saint Bartholomew's Eve in 1572, captured a breakdown of civil peace that was starker than anything since the brutal mass killing during the Albigensian Crusade of the early thirteenth century. France was divided in blood.

Yet, from 1494, having consolidated an unprecedented degree of control of France, successive warrior kings, Charles VIII (r. 1483–1498), Louis XII (r. 1498–1515), Francis I (r. 1515–1547) and Henry II (r. 1547–1559), launched themselves into a period of major warfare, notably in Italy, and competed first with the rulers of Spain and Austria, and then with the new Habsburg super-power in the person of the Emperor Charles V (r. 1519–1556). The kings benefited from the agricultural wealth of France and, in particular, from the land tax on those who lacked exemption due to their noble status, and from the salt tax. France's rulers displayed *gloire* (fame) and won prestige, as well as territory, notably Metz, Toul and Verdun, which fell to Henry II in 1552, while Charles was weakened by a Protestant rebellion in Germany.

On a longstanding pattern, the kings took a prominent role in command, and even combat. Thus, in the so-called 'Mad War' of 1485–88, in which leading aristocrats, backed by Austria and

England, opposed Charles VIII, he led an army against an aristocratic rebellion, and his presence helped lead rebel garrisons to surrender. The young Charles also led the invasion of Italy in 1494 and, on the retreat, also fought on the battlefield at Fornovo (1495). Louis XII took part in the successful cavalry attack on the Venetians at Agnadello (1509). Two years earlier, he had entered Genoa in full armour carrying a naked sword. In 1525, again in Italy, Francis I was captured at Pavia when the French were defeated by Charles V. He was then imprisoned until he agreed terms, only to reject them on his release.

WHILE THE LITERAL TRANSLATION OF *GLOIRE* **IS GLORY** it has a deeper meaning when applied to the French monarchy. The idea was that the monarch embodied France in physical terms and represented the soul of the country. The ability to project the glory and majesty of the monarchy's role was vital to its survival and reached its zenith with Louis XIV (r. 1643–1715) in the seventeenth and early eighteenth centuries. Some have suggested that Louis XVI (r. 1774–1792) lacked this, and that this played a vital role in his ultimate downfall.

Personal experience from their campaigning in Italy of the Renaissance was underlined by the purchase of Italian art, the first key figures in this regard being Charles VIII and Louis d'Orléans, later Louis XII. A determination to compete with other rulers encouraged the kings to patronize a version of the Renaissance in France. This was notably so with palace building or rebuilding in the Loire Valley, especially at Blois and Chambord. Le Clos Lucé in Amboise, the house where Francis accommodated Leonardo da Vinci from 1516 to 1519, can be visited. Ostentation operated at many levels, with Francis, in particular, very much developing the scale and splendour of the court and its activities.

At the same time, royal control within France faced challenges. Charles, Duke of Bourbon, the Constable of France, might have appeared an anachronism in 1523, when, in response to attempts by the royal family to gain his lands, he rebelled and turned to the Habsburgs. In the event, he did so without any serious loss to Francis and became a Habsburg general. Yet, from the 1560s to the 1620s, and again in the early 1650s, in the *Fronde* (two civil wars named after the French word for 'sling'), leading French nobles not only felt able to defy the Crown, but also inflicted great damage on it. A different form of challenge was posed by the beginning of the Protestant Reformation, which led to growing dissension in the 1540s and 1550s, in the face of repression of the Huguenots, as the French Protestants were known.

With Henry II defeated at Saint Quentin (1557) and at Gravelines (1558), bankrupt and alarmed by the spread of Protestantism, Philip II of Spain (r. 1556–1598) emerged the winner from the long wars with France. The Treaty of Cateau-Cambrésis in 1559 left him dominant in Italy, and that year also saw a jousting accident that led to Henry's death. Henry II's weak successors, his sons Francis II (r. 1559–1560), Charles IX (r. 1560–1574) and Henry III (r. 1574–1589), were unable to control the factionalism of the leading nobility, as the more decisive Henry II had done. This was a factionalism exacerbated by the growing struggle between Catholics and Huguenots, the former energized by the Counter-Reformation, which gathered pace from the 1550s and required the driving back of the Huguenots, who were Calvinists, looking to the nearby inspiration of Jean Calvin's Geneva.

In what became a protracted crisis of order and civil society, the French Wars of Religion were characterized by a collapse of royal authority, social strife and civil war. These wars lasted until the Edict of Nantes in 1598, resuming, on a smaller scale, during the reign of Louis XIII (1610–1643), and ending in royal victory in 1629. Open conflict broke out in 1560 with an unsuccessful Huguenot attempt to seize Francis II at Amboise. However, rather than a continuous period of warfare, let alone high-tempo campaigning, there was a series of distinct wars, separated by agreements and periods of peace that reflected a widespread desire for settlement, but set against the background of persistent differences and a high level of civil violence, so that years of peace were in reality uneasy armed truces.

The most prominent Catholic aristocrat, Francis, Duke of Guise, who was a veteran of the war with the Habsburgs and claimed descent from Charlemagne, soon broke the peace with the Huguenots, initiating a series of wars. On 1 March 1562, at Vassy, while travelling with large numbers of supporters, Guise became involved in a dispute with a Huguenot religious congregation that led to the massacre of the latter. In response, the Huguenot leader, the Prince of Condé, seized Orléans. The two sides fought at Dreux that December when Condé's advance on Paris was blocked. Heavy casualties, not least deaths and captures among the commanders at Dreux, and the assassination of Guise the following February, led to the Pacification of Amboise in March 1563, ending the First War of Religion. This had been a short war, shorter, for example, than the war with the League of the Public Weal of 1465–69, but it was serious because it was the first such civil conflict since the late fifteenth century, while the role of religion made a lasting compromise difficult, and indeed apparently impossible at this stage. New, destructive practices became the new norm.

Tensions indeed remained, with Huguenot fears that Charles IX would back Philip II of Spain, the most prominent Catholic ruler, leading to the outbreak of the indecisive Second War (1567–68), followed by the Third (1568–70). The one-sided nature of the Peace of Longjumeau at the close of the Second, requiring only the Huguenots to disarm, led directly to the pre-emptive strike that unleashed the next war. More generally, the inadequate enforcement of the various peace settlements was itself a cause of renewed conflict, while also being a reflection of the strength of distrust that was the basic background to the wars. Across France, civilians were involved in fighting, and both as perpetrators and as victims. There was a tendency to treat those of another religion as animals, which was used to justify their murder. Publications, and notably crude woodcuts that presented propaganda about atrocities committed by the other side, encouraged this attitude.

Cities now famous as tourist sites for other reasons saw bitter fighting in this period. In 1562, Rouen was stormed by the royal army and sacked for three days while a Huguenot mob damaged the Basilica of Saint Martin in Tours. In 1568 the walls of Chartres were breached by Huguenot cannon, but the attempt to storm the city was defeated and the breach sealed. There was conflict across France, as the rival religious groups and aristocratic factions were widely spread. At Viviers, the cathedral was plundered by Protestant soldiers in 1562 and the roof of the nave pulled down in 1567. The monastery at Vézelay was similarly assaulted.

The end of the Third War was followed by the admission of Admiral Gaspard de Coligny, the Huguenot leader, into the royal council. He sought to unite France behind a plan for attacking the Spaniards in the Low Countries where Protestantism was an important element in the rebellion against Philip II. Foreign policy was directly linked thereby to domestic politics. However, concern about Coligny's intentions and military preparations, especially from the king's influential mother, Catherine de' Medici, interacted with popular anti-Protestantism to create a volatile atmosphere. The unsuccessful attempted murder of Coligny on 22 August 1572, at the behest of Henry I, the new duke of Guise, led to fears of an imminent retaliation.

To pre-empt this, Charles IX and his council seem to have decided to murder Coligny and other Huguenot leaders. The Saint Bartholomew's Eve killing of leading Protestants, notably Coligny, on the night of 24 August, a lurid event by any standards, was followed by a widespread massacre of Paris's Huguenots by the Catholic populace. Carried out by civilians, the slaughter reflected the total breakdown of civic relations, with neighbours killing neighbours at close quarters. The slaughter was replicated in many other cities, such as Angers. The Pope struck a commemorative medal to celebrate the massacre, which was to be depicted by writers and artists, then and later, from Christopher Marlowe in his play *The Massacre at Paris* (1593), to Giacomo Meyerbeer's opera *Les Huguenots* (1836), which premiered with great success and was the first opera to be performed at the Paris Opéra more than a thousand times. The eighteenth-century writer Voltaire, who was appalled by the type of prejudice that led to the Saint Bartholomew's Eve massacre, claimed to be ill on its anniversary each year.

During the Wars of Religion, especially but not only in the towns (which were more politicized), there was a high level of engagement with the religious struggle. This engagement led to outbursts of mass violence, as well as to a degree of independence from aristocratic leadership, and among both the Catholic League and the Protestant towns. The massacre touched off the Fourth War (1572–73), rapidly followed by the Fifth (1574–76). A parallel politico-governmental system was established by the Huguenots: the 'Estates-General of the Provinces of the Said Union' with their (military) Protector. Arguments justifying resistance to the Crown were developed by Huguenot writers, for example the anonymous author of *Vindiciae contra tyrannos* (1579).

In each of these five conflicts, with lack of finance resulting in a steady decline in the size and effectiveness of the royal army as well as other armies, the royal army was unable to inflict a defeat on the Huguenots sufficient to transform the overall situation. Prominent aristocrats, however, were often governors of provinces where they had the centre of their landholdings and factional affinities, which gave them a number of mutually supporting ways in which to raise troops. Whereas, in the early wars, control of Paris was a central goal, after 1572 the Huguenots, with their key base at La Rochelle, were largely concerned to consolidate their position in the south and west. La Rochelle survived siege in 1573, and the Fifth War ended in 1576, with the royal army, bereft of funds, unable to set the terms for what became a compromise peace, which gave the Huguenots freedom of worship and the right to build churches and to garrison certain towns, a demonstration of the fragility of France as a unitary state. Catholic dissatisfaction with these terms undermined the peace settlement. In the Sixth War (1577), however, Henry III, Charles IX's brother and successor, lacked funds and success. He reached a settlement that accepted Protestant worship but limited the rights granted in 1576, which underlined the transience of such arrangements.

The years 1577–84 were less disruptive than the 1560s and early 1570s, but a high level of violence continued in the provinces, which led to the Seventh War (1579–80). Full-scale conflict resumed after the Protestant Henry of Navarre, the head of the House of Bourbon (which was descended from a fifth son of Louis IX), became heir to the throne in 1584 on the death of Francis, Duke of Anjou, Henry III's brother. Though baptized a Catholic, Henry of Navarre had been raised as a Protestant and only narrowly escaped death in the Saint Bartholomew's Eve massacre. The Catholic Henry I, the duke of Guise after Francis's assassination, and Philip II of Spain agreed to cooperate by the Treaty of Joinville, signed secretly in 1584, to thwart this succession. In 1585, during the 'War of the Three Henries' (i.e. King Henry III,

Henry of Guise and Henry of Navarre), the Catholic League, which the duke of Guise had founded in 1576, and which from 1585 to 1588 sided with Henry III, took over much of north and central France. Strong in the south, and with no incentive to compromise, the Huguenots fought on.

The Guise faction successfully intimidated Henry III, but their relationship deteriorated and, on the dramatic Day of the Barricades on 12 May 1588, Henry lost control of Paris to a pro-Guise rising and was left in control essentially of the Loire, Bordeaux and Dauphiné. In response, he had to make Guise Lieutenant-General of France, and the Estates-General meeting at Blois, Henry III's seat, backed Guise and not the king. Henry's desperate move in response – the murder of Guise at Blois on 23 December by his bodyguards (his brother, Louis Cardinal of Guise, was killed next day), which, reflecting the increasingly public nature of politics, was extensively covered in publications – did not solve the problem.

The Catholic League, now under Guise's brother Charles, Duke of Mayenne, turned completely against the king, with the *Parlement* of Paris in 1589 declaring the Cardinal of Bourbon, Henry of Navarre's Catholic uncle, king as Charles X. Weak and short of funds, Henry III felt it necessary to ally with the Protestant Henry of Navarre, and they jointly besieged Paris, only for Henry III to be assassinated by Jacques Clément, a Dominican lay brother. Before dying, Henry III recognized Henry of Navarre as his heir, but said he could only succeed if he became a Catholic. Henry III was the last of the Valois rulers.

As the war became more intense, Henry of Navarre benefited from victories over the Catholic League at Arques (1589) and Ivry (1590), where he led a crucial cavalry charge, but Paris survived a siege in 1590 thanks to relief by the impressive Spanish Army of Flanders under the Duke of Parma, which advanced from Belgium.

English forces intervened in support of Henry, only for the Spaniards under Parma to advance again and relieve besieged Rouen in 1592. Henry, nevertheless, was helped by his enemies' political divisions, not least over whether, after the death in 1590 of 'Charles X,' a Spaniard, Isabella Clara Eugenia (daughter of Philip II and of Henry II's eldest daughter, Elizabeth), was acceptable on the throne. The total lack of unified leadership on the side of the League was also important: in Paris in November 1591, Catholic radicals in the Council of Ten seized power, provoking, in reaction, a hostile show of force by Mayenne, which included the execution of some of his radical opponents and the takeover of the Paris militia, with soldiers of humble social status disarmed. This episode demonstrated the extent to which the Catholic cause was not socially united.

Henry's willingness to become a Catholic again in 1593 was important to winning allies, and helped lead to a political solution to the conflict, as did his preparedness to give large sums of money to key individuals. In 1594, he was crowned Henry IV in Chartres and entered Paris. This success was followed by a rapid increase in reconciliations with the king, with both aristocrats and town councils taking part. Mayenne, who had agreed a truce in July 1593, finally settled in October 1595. His son was made governor of the Île-de-France as part of the agreement, and he was given a substantial sum. In 1596, the League itself was dissolved.

Meanwhile, the war with Spain continued, and Spanish forces continued to intervene, especially in north-eastern France where they seized Calais and Amiens. There were also Spanish expeditions to Brittany, aimed against England, and to eastern France, designed to strengthen the Spanish position on the overland route, the so-called 'Spanish Road', from Lombardy to the Low Countries. Henry benefited greatly from Philip II also being at war with England and the Dutch and, in 1597, made his entry

I, TOP The Carnac Stones are a reminder of how much of France's deep history is pre-Roman, with a sophisticated society falling victim to Roman conquest.

II, ABOVE The Pont du Gard aqueduct is an impressive instance of what was a more widespread development of public infrastructure in the Roman centuries.

III, OPPOSITE Gregory of Tours's *Historia Francorum* was a key work in defining a sense of distinctiveness. The role of the Church in medieval French life was important as well as multifaceted.

IV, ABOVE Later representations of Joan of Arc, this from 1843, served both to provide an heroic account of French history and also one closely linked with Catholicism.

V, TOP *The Triumph of Henri IV* by Peter Paul Rubens, 1630. Trying to clothe France past and present in a Roman costume was an important source of legitimation.

VI, ABOVE *Aerial View of the Palace of Versailles* by Pierre Patel, 1668. Born in Picardy, Patel (1605–1676) worked in Paris and largely painted landscapes, often in a Classical style and some with biblical themes.

VII, OPPOSITE The west façade of Chartres cathedral: a Catholic eternal France.

VIII, TOP Jacques-Louis David was to paint the Revolution and Napoleon, in part using a Neoclassical style already developed under Louis XVI, as in *The Oath of the Horatii*, 1784.

IX, ABOVE The praying statues of Louis XVI and Marie Antoinette in the cathedral of Saint-Denis were part of the Restoration embrace of an ostentatious Catholicism.

x *The Consecration of the Emperor Napoleon*, 1805–7, by Jacques-Louis David captured the egocentric grandiloquence of the new imperial regime.

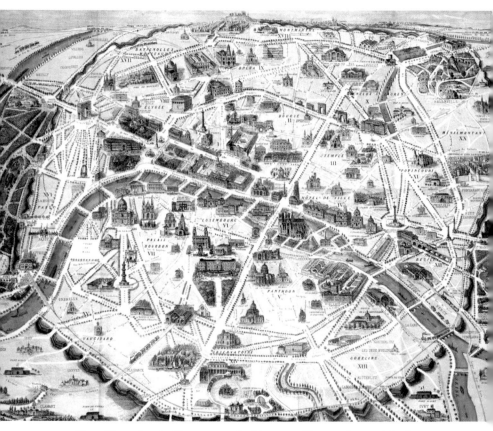

XI Plan of Paris after the Haussmann rebuilding, 1882. The site of most of the drama of French history from 1789 to 1871, Paris was repurposed as a new stage for power under Napoleon III.

into Amiens, on horseback, sceptre in hand, to watch the defeated Spanish garrison surrender. Conventionally, Spain's efforts were seen as failures, but the continued Spanish intervention helped force Henry to compromise with domestic opponents, which thus assisted Spain by keeping the French Crown weak.

The year 1598 brought peace: the last major League noble submitted, and on 13 April, with the Edict of Nantes, the Huguenots were granted liberty of conscience (effectively the freedom to hold their own beliefs), a measure of public worship, and the right to retain garrisons in many of the towns, *places de sûréte*, they occupied, including major cities such as Grenoble, La Rochelle, Montpellier and Nîmes. However, the role of Catholicism as the established religion was upheld and Protestants had to pay tithes. The concessions with the Huguenots, only about 6 per cent of the population, were to be eroded in the 1620s, and to be totally revoked in 1685 by Louis XIV in the Edict of Fontainebleau. In contrast, buying off the major Catholic aristocrats with a recognition of their provincial power-bases – in return for peace and their abandonment of alliance with Spain and of the more radical urban elements of the League – reflected the realities of power and laid out the prospectus of Bourbon monarchy.

The Peace of Vervins, signed on 2 May 1598, saw Philip II recognize Henry as King of France, withdraw his forces from France, and return Calais to France. This peace helped Henry strengthen his position against other opponents. Defeated by the French in 1600–1, with Mayenne now fighting for Henry, the Spanish ally Charles Emanuele, Duke of Savoy, was driven to accept the Treaty of Lyon in 1601. Under this, France gave up Saluzzo, but acquired Bugey, Valromey, Gex and Bresse, thus moving Savoy away from Lyon and the Rhône. This was to be a permanent gain for France, and enhanced the value of Henry II's ability to establish French power in the Lorraine region in 1552, which had underlined the vulnerability of its duke, while also giving the French Crown a greater interest in Alsace.

'Paris is worth a mass', a remark attributed to Henry, and certainly one that reflected the situation, was a testimony both to the importance of affirming the attributes of Catholic kingship in order to secure his position, not least in the face of opinion across society, and yet also to the reality of compromise, rather than the appearance of the heroic restoration of strong monarchy. It was unclear, however, whether the compromises of authority and power that characterized the establishment of Bourbon rule would not leave France lastingly weak and the tensions that faced France anew in the 1610s suggest that there is reason to believe that the Wars of Religion had left the country with serious problems.

The complex nature of power was well illustrated by the *lit de justice*: the occasion on which the king made a ceremonial visit to the *Parlement* of Paris and, with the monarch sitting on cushions on a dais, Jean du Tillet, its chief clerk from 1530 to 1570, emphasized the medieval roots of the ceremony, notably from the 1320s. In contrast, Tillet's work has been regarded as an exaggeration and an aspect of the more general search for the authentication and authority of age. Linked to this, it has been argued that the *lit de justice* became important only from 1537, while it was from 1597 that it became the occasion when the monarch enforced the registration of controversial legislation. Thus, in the tense and more adversarial situation of the sixteenth century, the *lit de justice* was a consequence of a distinctive constitutional practice focused on royal power or, at least, initiative.

An emphasis on politics can lead to an underplaying of other aspects of strain. The sixteenth century saw sustained population growth, but, as in England, that growth pressed on resources, contributing to significant inflation, notably in food prices, and particularly so by the closing decades. This social tension was a factor in the accentuation of concern about witchcraft. In his *De la démonomanie des sorciers* (1580), a much-reprinted manual for judges engaged in witchcraft cases, Jean Bodin (*c.* 1529–1596) applied legal concepts, classifying the evidence into a hierarchy of proofs and presumptions. Severe torture was to be used if necessary. Bodin's roving pen reflected the strains of society. In *La réponse de M. Jean Bodin aux paradoxes du Seigneur de Malestroit* (1568), he demonstrated the extent of inflation. In response to the chaos of civil war and the spread of resistance theory, Bodin, in his *République* (1576), pressed the need for undivided sovereignty, and later writers helped fashion this into the idea of the divine right of kings.

The Wars of Religion pushed national issues and alignments, rather than the politics of specific locations, to the fore. This was particularly apparent in the case of the cities, both Protestant and Catholic, but, at the same time, social tensions were also national. For the nobility, this was especially so over their status. They used the notion of *dérogeance*, or loss of status, to ensure that their privileges were regarded as incompatible with manual labour or retail trade; and thus underlined an exclusive character to nobility that could incorporate the older landed *noblesse d'épée* (nobility of the sword) and the more urban *noblesse de robe* (nobility of the robe), who were of more recent lineage and came from a legal background. Oligarchy was not new, but it was refashioned in the context of the economic, political and religious strains of the period.

6. From Henry IV
to Louis XIV, 1598–1715

Sunspots may well have been a key problem for seventeenth-century France. For, alongside heavy taxation, the public was hit hard by the strains of life, which were accentuated in the economic downturn of the seventeenth century that probably owed much to climate cooling. Agricultural productivity was under pressure, while the population, and therefore the size and working strength of the labour force, was affected by epidemics, including diseases that are rarely killers now, such as dysentery in 1706. The economic downturn pressed hard on the system of *métayage* (sharecropping) that affected most peasant tenure, with the landlord owning the land, stock and tools. Little was left for the peasant family, not least as taxes and tithes also had to be paid. Areas of rural industry offered the best livelihood, but peasants everywhere were hit hard by events such as damage from hunts. Moreover, they were obliged to provide unpaid labour for the lord and turn their mills and winepresses, while they were also exposed to the lords' powers of justice over their tenants. Unsurprisingly, social mobility was limited.

Problems in agriculture could lead to famine, as in 1693, and with savage and prolonged local impact. The number of deaths registered in the town of Albi jumped from 280 in 1708 to 967 in 1710 and, with births slumping from 357 to 191 and marriages from 100 to 49, recovery was slow. Economic activity remained low, municipal debts high, and houses abandoned, and, by 1750,

Albi had still not regained its population of 1700. War also hit the economy hard, accentuating the pressure on resources, as well as on the government's ability to operate. The shortage of food made the struggle with wild animals more serious, and near Abbeville in 1699, wolves regularly attacked sheep, while the wolves' heads and bears' paws displayed in Savoy were a testimony to a bitter struggle for control over Alpine grazing.

This was a grim context for the politics of the century. From the outset, despite peace in 1598, stability had remained precarious. Henry IV faced continued intervention by Spain, as well as opposition by prominent nobles. Indeed, the artillery was seen as sufficiently important by Henry's leading minister, Maximilian, Duke of Sully, for him to retain the post of *grand maître de l'artillerie* and the threat of bombardment led the rebel duke of Bouillon to surrender his fortified town of Sedan in 1606. Castles that could help resistance were destroyed or weakened, for example at Semur-en-Auxois in 1602 and at Les Baux-de-Provence in 1632.

Henry was assassinated by François Ravaillac, a fanatical Catholic, in Paris in 1610 en route to resume war with Spain. During his reign, he had been an opponent of Spanish interests abroad, a supporter of settlement in Canada, where Québec was established in 1608, and a developer of the economy at home. His monuments include the Pont Neuf, the Place des Vosges and the Grande Galerie of the Louvre. On the Pont Neuf is a bronze equestrian statue of Henry, commissioned in 1614, erected in 1618, destroyed in 1792 by Revolutionaries, and rebuilt in 1818.

The minority of Henry's infant son, Louis XIII (r. 1610–1643), saw renewed political instability, but also the extension of royal power in a way that resumed the long-term trend prior to the Wars of Religion. In 1614, control was imposed on Béarn, an independent territory that was a royal fief, but where Catholic worship was not permitted. The Estates had protested against an order to restore Catholic worship and all church property, whereupon the government resorted to the military option, which led to submission, not resistance, and Béarn was formally annexed to France.

In the 1620s the Wars of Religion resumed with successful campaigning against the Huguenots in 1620–22 and 1625–29. Commanded in person by Louis XIII, the successful siege of La Rochelle in 1627–28, with nearly half the population dying of starvation, demoralized the Huguenots, and further defeat in 1629, notably the sack of the town of Privas, led the Huguenots to accept royal terms. They were no longer to have the right to garrisons, and were thus dependent on the royal will. Unsuccessful English intervention ensured that the Huguenot challenge was intertwined with problems of foreign policy, just as aristocratic factionalism was to be linked to war with Spain in the 1630s, 1640s and 1650s.

The defeat of the Huguenots opened the way for a renewed integration of Crown and elite, and, alongside the role of force, there was a longer-term attenuation of Protestantism, especially among the nobility. This process owed much to social pressures and political opportunities. In the former, intermarriage was important, with mixed marriages leading to the bringing up of children in the dominant Catholicism. In the latter, nobles and others found that opportunities for royal patronage were in large part dependent on religion.

Meanwhile, in 1630, in the Day of the Dupes, Cardinal Richelieu (1582–1642), Louis XIII's chief minister from 1624, consolidated his control of the court and ministry, outwitting his opponents. Richelieu was an aristocrat who had become a bishop and risen at court, and who understood the crucial need to work with Louis. The consolidation of his power affected the arts. Rubens's *The Triumph of Henri IV* (1630, see pl. v) was intended for the gallery devoted to him in the Luxembourg Palace in Paris, but neither painting nor gallery were finished due to the disgracing of Henry's widow, Marie de' Medici, for her opposition to Richelieu. The sketch depicted Henry entering Paris in a chariot crowned by a winged figure in the manner of a Classical Roman triumph. In comparison, Louis XIII was not an impressive leader, but he was depicted as a great heroic figure, and compared to Alexander the Great and Hannibal. Engravings were matched by pamphlets emphasizing his successes.

Although under threat from repeated conspiracies, Richelieu, an adroit manoeuvrer, retained control until his death when he was succeeded by his Italian-born protégé, Cardinal Mazarin, who held this position until his death in 1661. These years saw conflict with the Habsburgs of Spain and Austria, and domestic opposition, notably by nobles, for much of the nobility was hostile toward royal favour for the cardinals and their allies. Gaston, Duke of Orléans, the brother of Louis XIII and, until the birth of the future Louis XIV in 1638, his heir, was an independent political figure, able to raise forces and willing to conspire against Richelieu and even the Crown. Government measures such as attempts to limit duels were very unpopular with the elite. So also was the destruction of fortifications that had resisted royal troops, as with part of the château of Amboise in 1631 as a result of rebellion by Gaston.

Under the pressure of war taxation, there were also peasant uprisings, notably in Gascony in 1636–37 and in Normandy in 1639. The Gascony rebels appeared a threat because they had muskets and gunpowder, were led by some local gentry, and included in their ranks veterans of the siege of La Rochelle. These risings had to be suppressed by large organized forces. Richelieu was subsequently to be seen as a key figure in the making of France but, at the time, his position appeared as precarious as that of the state. Moreover, in 1636, Spanish forces invading from Belgium toward

Paris got as far as Corbie and Roye, both of which fell. Conspiracies against Richelieu continued until the end of his ministry, those of the Count of Soissons and the Marquis of Cinq-Mars in 1641 and 1642 respectively.

Meanwhile, French forces made significant gains. The exploitation of the Catalan rising against Spain in 1640 permitted the conquest of the in-between province of Roussillon, the fortress-city of Perpignan falling in 1642. In the Low Countries, Arras was captured in 1640. Outside Europe, bases were developed in the West Indies, notably Guadeloupe, Dominica, Martinique and Cayenne in 1635, while Saint-Louis on the mouth of the River Senegal was established in 1638.

The *Fronde*, the series of civil wars which indicated a serious breakdown in the political process, followed in 1648–53. They reflected a combination of unease over the political complexion of the Mazarin ministry, the burdens arising from war, and the general atmosphere of strain derived from the demographic and economic crises of the period which, variously, included falling agricultural production and disease. Domestic tensions channelled and exacerbated the role of foreign war in creating policy disputes and financial pressures. The crisis led to civil war as well as constitutional moves, including an assembly of nobles in 1651 and talk of calling an Estates-General. There was not a religious dimension, for the Huguenots remained quiescent. However, a *Fronde parlementaire*, focusing on Paris and opposition by the *Parlement* of Paris, was followed by the princely *Fronde* in 1650–51, and then the 'Spanish *Fronde*' from late 1651 led by Louis, Prince of Condé, the 'Great Condé'. The *frondeurs* had to be beaten in battle, notably at Saint-Antoine in the suburbs of Paris in 1652, and it is unclear what would have happened but for these victories, not least because the Spaniards continued their support for the *frondeurs*, particularly Condé, and remained resilient until 1658–59.

However, a radical movement in Bordeaux, the *Ormée*, had very few members, and a Spanish attempt to intervene by invading Gascony to help it failed. The *Fronde* proved more useful to Spain in permitting the reconquest of Catalonia.

By the time the *Fronde* began, the bulk of the senior clergy and the *noblesse de robe* accepted the inviolability of the king, but the *noblesse d'épée* were less well persuaded and, partly in consequence, readier to defy the cardinal-ministers in the 1630s to 1650s. Subsequently, the shared benefits offered to officers in the expanded royal armies proved effective alongside the indoctrination that had been provided by education. The underlying resilience of the aristocratic order emerged. Thus, in Aix, old and new aristocratic families were readily assimilated in a reasonably fluid social structure as the city offered a variety of sources of income and investment, especially the opportunity to purchase office, to old and new families alike. Far from there being clear divides within the elite, divides, notably between the *noblesse d'épée* and the *noblesse de robe*, that would have weakened it, instead old families bought offices to nearly the same extent as new families, and they invested in bonds even more. Conversely, those successful in the towns purchased fiefs and acquired titles, and thus both expanded their landed profile and accommodated themselves to the landed order. Political division in this context was based on factions and politics, not functions. Marriage enabled aristocratic factionalism, but also promoted assimilation and kept the social structure flexible.

Conventionally, France under Richelieu and Mazarin has been seen as a state with a synergy of war, military expansion and development of state power; but that approach has been dismantled by scholars. Rather than war acting as an enabler for state growth, it was a heavy burden that consistently encouraged a government of expedients to match the politics of opportunism. Moreover, far from there being a seamless process of victory and expansion, as can be suggested by a selection of brief headline events, the war proved very difficult. The end of the *Fronde* brought little improvement, and while, in 1654, a Spanish attempt to regain Arras was defeated, the Spaniards captured Rocroi, a step that is scarcely ever mentioned, in contrast to the much-celebrated French victory there over a Spanish army in 1643. Resource issues pressed on the French, greatly affecting the operation of the government, while serious defeats at Pavia (1655) and Valenciennes (1656) led France to offer reasonable peace terms, only for Philip IV of Spain to reject them. In 1658, in contrast, English intervention on the side of France brought victory outside Dunkirk over the outnumbered Spaniards in the Battle of the Dunes. After the battle, Dunkirk fell and French successes in Flanders encouraged Spain to terms.

The war that had begun in 1635, with a precursor in 1628–31, ended in the Peace of the Pyrenees of 7 November 1659, with France gaining Artois, a number of Flemish towns and Roussillon. In return, France abandoned its claim to Barcelona and its support for Portugal. Moreover, the treaty stipulated the marriage of Louis XIV to Maria Theresa, the daughter of Philip IV of Spain, which gave Louis a claim on the Spanish succession because the dowry to be paid in return for renouncing her claim to the throne was not delivered.

Various religious groups were closely associated with the politics of diplomacy and faction, with the *dévots* (the devout) the party hostile to Protestantism at home and abroad. More generally, the Counter-Reformation remained a vital force. Thus, alongside Richelieu and Mazarin – both of whom were willing to ally with Protestant powers, such as the Dutch and Sweden, against fellow Catholics, notably the Habsburgs – were Catholic activists such as Vincent de Paul (1581–1660), a key *dévot*, who founded the Lazarist

Mission, or the Congregation of the Mission, which was designed to help the people in smaller settlements. The Oratory, founded in 1611 by Pierre de Bérulle (1575–1629), a Jesuit pupil, was intended to increase the role and calibre of parish priests. Established in 1630, the Company of the Blessed Sacrament was a very well-connected secret Catholic confraternity that sought to strengthen the Church, to provide charity, and to attack Protestantism. At the same time, there was Catholic resistance in France to Papal authority in the shape of Gallicanism (i.e. support for the Church of France), which asserted its claims against Ultramontanism, which looked 'beyond the mountains' towards Rome and supported Papal pretensions towards the universal control of Catholicism. While the continued presence of the Huguenots left the situation uncertain, the French Catholic Church was embedding itself into the political, social and cultural structures of France.

Born in 1638, Louis XIV (r. 1643–1715) assumed his royal authority with the death of Mazarin in 1661 and began with a dramatic demonstration of his authority. Nicolas Fouquet, Mazarin's protégé who was the Superintendent of Finances and the builder of Vaux-le-Vicomte, a palace that Louis envied, was disgraced and imprisoned until his death. Fouquet plays a heroic role in Alexandre Dumas's novel *The Vicomte de Bragelonne* (1847–50).

Crucially, Louis renewed harmonious relations with the social elite. These had been lost under the rule of the cardinal-ministers who had clearly courted only the support of the section of the elite that was willing to back them, and had therefore compromised the idea that the Crown should reach out to all the nobility. The cardinal-ministers had also suffered from their inability to bring France's long conflict with Spain to a victorious end, or to any end prior to the peace of 1659. In reality, this was a peace of exhaustion as much as victory, though the treaty is conventionally presented in that light.

Louis's fundamental conservatism can be grasped by contrasting him with the more radical Peter the Great of Russia (r. 1682–1725). Louis's broad-based cooperation with the nobility, rather than any supposed 'Absolutist' agenda of centralization and bureaucratization, brought stability to France and represented a revival of the Renaissance monarchy of the early sixteenth century. At the same time, Louis's approach to governing helped ensure a more powerful state than the earlier version, not least in its ability to tax, and by increasing the size of both army and navy. By the 1690s, testifying to aristocratic confidence in Louis, over 20,000 nobles were serving in the military, which was of unprecedented size for France.

Studies of Provence and Languedoc indicate that the nobility in the first half of the seventeenth century sought to prevent a further extension of royal authority, in part in response to the unpopularity of the Richelieu and Mazarin ministries. In contrast, from the 1660s, in these provinces and elsewhere, there was an accommodation of the state-building programmes of the central government and the local interests of the nobility. Likewise with towns, which preferred stability to disorder, and were ready to become part of a system of accommodation. This accommodation has led some scholars to present Absolutism – the total power of the monarch – as an anachronistic historical construct imposed on the period by later generations championing false patterns and failing to appreciate the reality of compromise. At the same time, this revisionist interpretation has been contested, and royal authority has been presented in terms of a harsh reality of expropriation and lack of consultation.

The stress usually placed on Louis's deployment of *intendants* – powerful officials sent to exercise governmental functions in the provinces – can hide the fact that they had only small staffs, that they had to cooperate with local institutions, such as provincial

Parlements, and that they had to defer to the power of the *gouverneurs* of provinces, who were major aristocrats. That situation did not prevent the conservatively minded Louis from being responsible for change, not least through increasing the size of the army and raising peacetime taxation to pay for it. The *intendants* therefore essentially complemented existing mechanisms in serving the traditional financial and military needs of the Crown. They represented neither a major administrative transformation nor an agency of despotic power and centralization. Indeed, given the scale of purchase of government offices (venality), and hereditary nature of offices, the extent to which the 'state' was subject to the will of the ruler, as the traditional emphasis on *intendants* might imply, is doubly questionable.

The sale of offices by the Crown was particularly important in France and represented a way to tap the wealth of those who otherwise made at best a limited financial contribution to the costs of the state, as a result of tax exemptions. Ironically, many of the offices, in turn, brought new exemptions. As with tax farming, the sale of offices represented a way for the Crown to obtain money at once, but at the cost of future revenues and by diverting investment income from the productive economy. More positively, the sale of office was a means of raising revenue from the prominent rather than taxing them indirectly by means of their reduced capacity to earn rental income as a result of the taxation of their peasant tenants. Venality of office encapsulated a world of shared Crown–elite interests that, despite serious strains, was held together by the exchange of status for service, which was a crucial form of government and of political stability.

Nobles no longer controlled private armies, as during the Wars of Religion, but their major role in the royal army remained one of considerable and practised autonomy, which was an aspect of the reconceptualization of private–public arrangements that existed as part of what has been termed Absolutism. These arrangements were an important means of royal power and authority in this system, and yet also a limitation of them. Because the expansion of governmental military strength was a matter largely of co-opting elites, rather than coercing them, it proved difficult to limit unofficial military activity. More positively, military entrepreneurship could be redirected through more regular military channels, notably thanks to the system and ethos of the aristocratic proprietorship of regiments. It proved far harder, however, to suppress feuds, brigandage and duels enjoying elite support, while there were also problems with the co-option of elites. Thus, a 1678 English memoir on French resources suggested that, although the army had 265,000 troops listed as in pay, at least a fifth 'may be deducted by false musters and other devices of officers, notwithstanding all the great rigour used against those that are found faulty'.

Moreover, aristocratic generals played a major role in policy, and not always a helpful one. Aristocrats were important at court, where life brought them together with the monarch and royal splendour helped elicit aristocratic cooperation and consent. Thus, court ballets provided aristocratic civility at the behest of the Crown, while hunting offered a different form of sociability. Most nobles did not have this close relationship with the court and, instead, spent their time on their estates, but they would be linked to the court through the social and patronage affinities that aligned noble society and linked the centre to the regions.

With the exception of the unsuccessful Huguenot Camisards in the Cévennes region of southern France in 1702–4, 1675 was the last year of large-scale revolts in France prior to the outbreak of the Revolution in 1789. Troops suppressed revolts in the Boulogne region in 1662, the Vivarais in 1670, and Bordeaux and Brittany in 1675, and the Marquise de Sévigné referred to the Breton trees as bowed to one side because of the weight of the large number of peasants hanged when the rising was suppressed by troops. Paris had defied and expelled royal forces in 1588 and 1648 but, thereafter, did not do so again until 1789.

The Cévennes insurrection by the Huguenots against forcible conversion followed the Revocation of the Edict of Nantes by the Edict of Fontainebleau in 1685, a process that involved great brutality by royal troops, including much sadism. Both sides responded to religious antagonism by killing prisoners, and there was murderous repression by royal troops. This rising occurred during the War of the Spanish Succession (1701–14), but France's opponents were unable to send effective help to this inland region, although Britain, with its naval presence in the Mediterranean, tried to do so. The penal restrictions on the Huguenots were not relaxed until 1787.

The Cévennes rising, however, was in a marginal area low in population and not, like the *Fronde*, in major centres. Indeed, Louis's reign as an adult did not see the precariousness and crises that had characterized those of his grandfather, Henry IV, his father, Louis XIII, and his own minority. Thanks to the creation of an important measure of domestic stability under Louis XIV, the minority of his successor, his great-grandson Louis XV (r. 1715–1774), was less disturbed than his own or that of Louis XIII. Indeed, Louis XIV's successors inherited an impressive political legacy. Whereas the regimes of the nineteenth century had a precarious background until the Third Republic was reasonably well-grounded in the 1890s, the situation in the eighteenth century was initially far better.

Europe was awed by Louis XIV's strength and frightened by his actual and supposed ambitions. As the result of a series of wars, he advanced France's boundaries, although at considerable cost, which attracted criticism within France in his later years as he became less successful. Earlier, there had been widespread support for his dynastic and territorial aggrandizement, and war was so much an inherent pillar of state power that, in 1734, Louis's surviving grandson, Philip V of Spain, told the French envoy that war was necessary for the political stability of the French monarchy. He might have added successful war, and the lesson of French history was to bear out this observation.

From the outset, Louis introduced a marked tone of bellicosity into policy. His first war, that of Devolution (1667–68), was a relatively modest affair, motivated by an opportunistic claim to part of the Spanish succession. Under Condé, who had received Louis's forgiveness after the Peace of the Pyrenees, and Henri, Viscount Turenne, the French conquered Franche-Comté and Flanders. Under pressure from the threat of intervention by the Dutch and English, Louis accepted terms in 1668, returning Franche-Comté but keeping Lille and Tournai. The War of Devolution was short-lived as well as successful but, to put this in context, these gains were far less than those won by Russia at the expense of Poland in 1667, although that reflected the presence in western Europe of a number of second-rank powers able and willing to combine against any potentially dominant force, and thus to restrict its growth.

Angered by their opposition to his expansion, and their republicanism, Louis isolated the Dutch before attacking them in 1672, only being stopped when the Dutch breached their dykes. Having won a quick triumph, however, Louis had little sense of how the war would develop diplomatically and militarily. The Dutch offered terms, but Louis issued excessive demands, including for major territorial gains and the acceptance of Catholic worship, for he was determined to gain prestige by being seen as the champion of Catholicism, supplanting the Habsburgs in this role. The war then changed shape, in part because of Louis's overconfidence and maladroit handling of others, but also because the coalition he had assembled to support his aggression was unstable. England abandoned him in 1674, while the Holy Roman Emperor Leopold I (r. 1658–1705) went to war against France. The conflict went on without French forces able to deliver victory, while the taxes raised to deal with the costs of the war helped cause the risings of 1675.

Yet, the Dutch War closed with the Treaty of Nijmegen of 1678, under which Louis gained Franche-Comté, Freiburg, Bouillon and more of the Spanish Netherlands. Although the war did not lead to the crushing defeat of the Dutch that Louis had anticipated, there was enough success and glory to satisfy his pride and to encourage the sense that, while he could not dictate events, Louis was the leading ruler in Christian Europe. There was increasingly a bullying tone to his diplomatic stance, as in 1684 when, without any declaration of war, about 13,000 cannonballs were fired at Genoa by the French fleet, in order to move its alliance away from Spain. There was also expansion outside Europe, notably bases in India-Surat (1667) and Pondicherry (1674), and in West Africa-Gorée (1674). Louisiana followed from 1699.

Thanks to his aggression, Louis helped to give France its essential modern shape, notably on the north-eastern, eastern and southern frontiers. Due to his gains, cities such as Besançon, Dunkirk, Lille, Perpignan and Strasbourg became possessions of the French Crown, even if the process of Frenchification was frequently drawn-out and it encountered much opposition in some areas, such as Franche-Comté, Lille and, even more, Strasbourg, which was gained in 1681.

The new possessions were fortified at considerable cost, with new-style fortifications designed by Sébastien Le Prestre de Vauban, a master of siegecraft as well as fortification. Richelieu, in his *Testament Politique* (1688), had advocated entrenching frontiers by means of fortifications. Under Louis XIII, there were major fortifications, as at Pinerolo on the Alpine frontier, while the fortress at the entrance to Lorient harbour, renamed Port Louis, was rebuilt and strengthened by Marshal Brissac, with five new bastions added in 1616–22 and the citadel completed in 1637 by a demi-lune. However, there was nothing that compared with the systematic attempt to defend vulnerable frontier regions seen under Louis XIV, in particular a double line of fortresses to defend the north-eastern frontier. This reflected geopolitical factors, notably the proximity to Paris of hostile powers based in modern Belgium, the high population density of the frontier region, a good resource base, excellent river communications, and the challenge posed by the Spanish forces that advanced into France in 1636, which led to a determination to block any recurrence. Appointed Commissioner General of Fortifications in 1678, Vauban supervised the construction of thirty-three new fortresses, such as those at Arras, Ath, Blaye, Briançon, Lille, Mont-Dauphin, Mont-Louis and New Breisach, and the renovation of many more, as at Belfort, Besançon, Landau, Montmédy, Sisteron, Strasbourg and Tournai. These fortifications can be readily seen, for example at Arras, Bayonne, Blaye, Fort Médoc, Lille, Montreuil-sur-Mer and Villefranche-de-Conflent. They are much more than remains: Belfort, for example, still has an impressive and working fortress and Camaret-sur-Mer is an evocative example of a sea fort.

These fortresses proved of lasting worth. Captured from Spain by France in 1667 in a siege directed by Vauban, and retained under the Peace of Aix-la-Chapelle in 1668, Lille was refortified by him. Four hundred men worked on the citadel for three years, creating a base for 1,200 troops. The principal entrance, the Place Royale, was built at an angle to the drawbridge to avoid direct hits. Although it was to fall to the British in 1708 (being returned at the subsequent peace), the still-impressive citadel was not taken in 1744 or 1792 by the British and Austrians respectively. In 1940, the firm, albeit ultimately unsuccessful, defence of Lille delayed the German advance toward the English Channel, providing more opportunity for the evacuation of British and French forces from Dunkirk.

In essence, Vauban's skilful use of the bastion and of enfilading fire represented a continuation of already familiar techniques that looked back to before the age of gunpowder. He placed the main burden of the defence on the combination of fortifications and artillery, again not a new approach. Instead, it was the crucial ability of the French state to fund such a massive programme that was novel. For example, New Breisach, built to control an important Rhine crossing and to offer a route into southern Germany, cost nearly three million livres to construct between 1698 and 1705. Vauban also played a role in the fortification of naval bases, notably Brest, Toulon and Rochefort, an aspect of the major build-up of the navy under Louis. France, for a while, had the largest navy in the world. French mastery was also shown in siegecraft, as at Dôle and Besançon.

There was a 'show' aspect to Vauban's fortifications, while Louis's triumphs, such as the contested crossing of the Rhine in 1672 and the sieges of Maastricht (1673), Ghent (1678), Mons (1691) and Namur (1692), were all celebrated with religious services, commemorative displays and paintings, as with Charles Le Brun's 1678–79 painting *The Second Conquest of the Franche-Comté, 1674*. Louis also appeared as a warrior in works of art that had a different theme, for example Le Brun's *The Resurrection of Christ* (1674). Louis sponsored splendour as a setting for his kingship, and notably so at Versailles, the palace begun in 1664 that proclaimed his power (see pl. VI). In the Salon de la Guerre, finished in 1686, Antoine Coysevox presented Louis as a stuccoed Mars, the God of War.

In addition, building in Paris itself during Louis's reign – with its repertoire of royal column, triumphal arch and monumental avenue – was designed to enhance the splendour of the monarchy as well as the capital. The expansion of Paris was marked by the building of royal palaces and by major projects, including the Luxembourg Palace, the Palais-Royal, the Institute de France, the Observatoire and the Invalides. The visiting William Mildway observed of the squares of Paris:

> that of Vendôme especially has an air of the utmost magnificence. In the middle of it is a large equestrian statue of Louis the 14th with a pompous inscription. Another statue of him is fixed in the Place de Victoire, on a pedestal, Victory holding a crown of laurel over his head, and under his feet lie four statues chained representing four different nations which it is pretended he brought under his subjection. And indeed all the gates of the city are only so many triumphal arches erected to his honour, on each of which the chiefest heroical acts of his reign are represented in fine basso relievo.

In royal iconography, the monarchy symbolized France. This symbolization and ideological centrality was pushed hard during this reign, but became less credible thereafter. Artifice played a major role in the creation of the image of Louis, a process eased by the absence in this period of anything equivalent to subsequent cults of sincerity. The monarch became the centre of a cult of ornamental heroism, while honour, a key theme in social position and a means to preserve social cohesion, became fundamental to a more structured environment of royal display than existed under Henry IV.

The honour of France also looked back, with a strong interest in mapping the past in French circles, partly because this was of direct relevance to Bourbon attempts to use historical claims to justify expansionism and partly because of a more long-term

interest in history that reflected the increase in national consciousness among the elite. Thus, Nicolas Sanson offered geographical
commentaries on Caesar's Gallic wars, and his maps included
Galliae antiquae (1642) and *Gallia vetus ex C. Julii Caesaris com-
mentariis descripta* (1649). Mapmaker Bercy in about 1680 produced
a map of France under Clovis that appeared in two editions.

Yet, there was also a shift in the style of power. Louis's image
changed in his later years, with a new reliance not on allegorical
themes, but on a closer engagement with issues of policy, which
was an aspect of a growing interest in reason as a justification of
policy. Aristocratic constitutionalism in the 1700s was an aspect
of the same, but to a different purpose as it pressed for a government and society based upon Christian ideals. The aspirations
and plans of Chevreuse, Fénelon, Saint-Simon and Beauvilliers,
all aristocrats, required an absolute monarch willing to modify the
government. While hoping that a revival of cooperation between
king and people could be obtained through consultation, most
still wanted a paternalist king who retained ultimate power.

Another element in this very varied 'proto-Enlightenment'
was the emphasis on logic derived from the mathematical and
philosophical work of René Descartes (1596–1650). Drawing
heavily on deductive reasoning and mathematical abstraction,
in accordance with his *Discours de la méthode* (1637), Descartes
emphasized motion in the universe, notably in his *Principes de
la philosophie* (1644). The stress on a mechanized cosmos was also
seen in the *Institutio astronomica* (1647) of the mathematician
Pierre Gassendi (1592–1655). Descartes's whirlpool theories of
space, as being composed of vortices of matter and of gravitation
acting accordingly, were to be refuted by Isaac Newton, but there
was a common emphasis on regular and predictable processes
and forces. In 1667, the Paris Observatory was established. Work
by its head, Jean-Dominique Cassini, made it possible to predict

the eclipses of Jupiter's satellites, and thus to determine longitude on land. The Planisphère Terrestre, a physical space laid out by Cassini in the Observatory to coordinate the astronomical information coming in from correspondents and to record accurately the geographical details of the Earth, appeared in a printed version in 1696.

There were other significant intellectual developments. Bernard Le Bovier de Fontenelle (1657–1757) defended the Moderns against the Ancients in his *Digression sur les anciens et les modernes* (1688) and presented an account of the nature of the universe – *Entretiens sur la pluralité des mondes* (1686) – as well as a *Histoire des oracles* (1687) and *De l'origine des fables* (1724), a rational assessment of the creation and spread of myths.

Art cannot be so readily fitted into this model, but it saw significant developments, notably in that of a distinctive French Classicism that was different to the more exuberant and less static Italian Baroque, even though there were also links between them. Nicolas Poussin and Claude Lorrain produced mythological paintings that had parallels in Italy, but, in architecture, the contrast was clearer, notably with the work of Louis Le Vau and, later, Jules Hardouin-Mansart. Classicism was very much seen through the east façade of the Louvre and also with Versailles. The royal imprimatur was more generally significant: the music of Jean-Baptiste Lully and the plays by Pierre Corneille and Jean-Baptiste Molière were sponsored by the state. The Church was also a major patron: Jesuit colleges date from this period, as do major churches.

The difficulty of fitting all these elements into a common pattern of development is encapsulated in the case of Jansenism, which emphasized the need to keep religion in the picture after the Wars of Religion and to retain its mysteries instead of treating it as a rational phenomenon. Originally an early seventeenth-century theological movement, Jansenism restated Augustinian notions and called into question the ability of man to achieve salvation by his own efforts, instead insisting that God's gift was beyond human understanding. Louis, who sought uniformity in French religious life, was unhappy about a belief that denied the ability of secular and ecclesiastical authorities to represent God's infallible will. He was also unhappy about the division this belief created within Catholicism.

In alliance with the Papacy, action against the Jansenists was stepped up in the 1700s, but this alliance aroused opposition both in the French Church and in the *Parlement* of Paris, each of which defended national Gallican privileges in the face of the universal pretensions of the Papacy. Jansenism provided a battleground for a Catholic country now more concerned about the respective realms of Papal, episcopal and *parlementaire* authority than the challenge posed by a weak French Protestantism. Related issues went on being highly significant until the 1760s.

Economic developments during the century included the building of canals. The Briare canal built in 1604–42 and the Orléans one that followed in 1676–92 were to help link the Seine and Loire river systems, while the Canal du Midi, originally named the Canal Royal en Languedoc, from Toulouse to the Étang de Thau close to the Mediterranean, was constructed in 1666–81. Henry IV, Richelieu and Louis XIV sponsored initiatives, notably in foreign trade and the establishment of factories. Such economic interventionism, known as mercantilism, was particularly associated with Jean-Baptiste Colbert and the state-controlled charges he sought to enable France to compete economically with the Dutch. Colbert, the Controller-General of Finances from 1665 and Secretary of State of the Navy from 1669, both until his death in 1683, wanted production quantified so as to help him understand and thereby be able to manage developments, and, to that

end, established a corps of inspectors designed to provide information about manufacturing and to implement royal decrees.
His initiatives in the 1660s were to be significant to the development of a longstanding statistical basis in French government, a
basis that allowed for the pursuit of informed policies of change.
In 1663, royal officials in the provinces were instructed to compile
information about their areas, a means of control very different
from royal visits and the related personal links. In addition, the
mapping of France was taken forward by the use of more effective surveying and astronomical methods, but, begun in 1679,
surveying by Jean Picard and Philippe de La Hire led to a map
that revealed that France was much smaller than had been previously believed because the coastline had been plotted too far
into the sea.

Alongside improvement there were continuing problems.
Thus, the government's manipulation of financial mechanisms
in order to obtain credit was but part of a broader set of problems.
Any consideration of details reveals the extent to which the government had fewer resources than its pretensions would suggest. For
example, delays in the striking and delivery of new coins by the
Paris mint led in 1701 to the issue of certificates, known as *billets
de monnoye*, to the owners of old coins and bullion delivered for
recoinage. These were over-issued and consequently depreciated
in value. Inadequate revenues led to the need to finance the War
of the Spanish Succession (1701–14) by borrowing and issuing bills
on other agencies involved in royal finance, such as the Receivers-
General and the General Tax Farmers. By 1708, the total raised
this way had reached about 800 million livres and the *billets de
monnoye* were partly repudiated by converting that 800 million
into 250 million livres of *billets de l'état*, but confidence in the new
billets, as in their predecessors, was limited by the government's
refusal to accept them as payment for taxes, although it used them

to pay bills. The fluctuating value of these units of paper currency hampered trade, and general confidence was further lessened by the government's capital debt, although suggestions of a default were not pursued. In this and other instances, the policy means available to the government were limited.

So, more fundamentally, were the cultural resources for economic growth. Rulers living at Versailles, with its symbolic demands, were much less exposed to the dynamic forces of economic life and overseas activities than a government and Parliament located in London, the growing centre of world trade and finance. Although, taken together, the various French ports were extremely active and the Loire alive with the sails of river vessels, the concentration of both politics and trade in London was not matched in Paris. Instead, the scale of French agriculture gave a character to France as well as bringing an underlying strength to the economy and to public finances, and supporting a population that was greater in size than that of any other state in western or central Europe. Moreover, the size of this population provided an essential ability to deploy large armies, as well as the navy.

These strengths, however, helped lead to a degree of hubris on the part of Louis, and this hubris ensured that his reign ended up as a morality tale about overstretch and the need to understand limits. This was the case in terms of war, international relations, ecclesiastical harmony, the economy and finances. Growing difficulties more obviously characterized his reign from the late 1680s. Most sadly for Louis, this was also the case with his family, his son, Louis, the Dauphin, eldest grandson, Louis, Duke of Burgundy, and eldest surviving great-grandson, Louis, Duke of Brittany, all falling victim to smallpox or measles in 1711–12. Again, that underlined unpredictability, as did the threatened demise of the young soon-to-be Louis XV, from measles in 1712 and while as yet a childless king from smallpox in 1728, which threatened to lead to the dynastic union of France and Spain in the person of Louis XIV's second grandson, Philip V of Spain.

France's position in Europe had not matched Louis's iconography. Whatever its many strengths, France was unable even to secure the defeat of the isolated Dutch in 1672, let alone to operate further afield with sustained success. Dominance of neighbouring areas in the Spanish Netherlands (Belgium), and (less consistently) the Rhineland, was not an indicator of a wider military or diplomatic capability. Thus, in 1675–76, an attempt to undermine the Spanish position in Sicily failed. Moreover, French success in the Nine Years War (1688–97) was more limited than in the Dutch War, while France suffered heavily in the War of the Spanish Succession, being driven from Germany and Italy after defeats at Blenheim (1704) and Turin (1706) respectively. Territorial gains under Louis did not lead to a major shift in geopolitics, and the possibility of French hegemony, which Louis's opponents emphasized when they sought to encourage opposition to his policies, was unlikely; such hegemony was only practicable if, as with the Franks under Charlemagne, other Christian powers were very weak and divided. In the early 1680s, with Austria threatened by the Turks, and England disunited, French dominance appeared a threat to the independence of the rest of Europe, but it was blocked in the late 1680s and swept aside in the 1700s. Nevertheless, if the kingdom was not quite the powerhouse Louis hoped it to be, the concept of 'France', more or less controlled by one ruler, was now established within its own people more than ever before.

Climate change had brought famine in a deeply unequal agricultural society, but the seventeenth century saw some development, not least the foundation of an overseas empire. France was home to very diverse cultural and linguistic groups: even a physical barrier such as the Pyrenees proved permeable to ties of sympathy and language between Basque and Catalan, while along the newly redefined eastern borders there were even more pronounced and durable links. But there and elsewhere, the country was divided also by religious differences which the state could only partly repress or conceal. Despite these enduring challenges, the Bourbon version of a sacral monarchy had at length managed to create a hexagonal France recognizable to modern eyes. The challenge was to make it endure and develop.

7. The *Ancien Régime,* 1715–1789

Was the Revolution inevitable? The increasingly accurate maps of the period, notably the Turgot Plan of Paris of 1734–36, make the country seem less distant from today as familiar sites come into view, but society was very different, being massively inegalitarian by social group, as well as by gender, and, from the modern perspective, such inegalitarianism can make revolution appear inevitable. Yet, eighteenth-century France is only in the shadow of the Revolution that began in 1789 if you look backwards from the present. In practice, to shape the history of the period in terms of what eventually happened is to do violence to contemporary views. Indeed, there was no sense that revolution was inevitable, and, by European standards, France was not particularly unequal nor unstable, and Russia and the lands of the Austrian Habsburgs were both more so. Monarchical propaganda, indeed, emphasized a positive view of France. Thus, the *Atlas historique et géographique de la France* (1764), the first of its type, presented contemporary France under the title 'La France Renaissante sous le Règne heureux de Louis XV le Bien-Aimé' (France Reborn under the Happy Reign of Louis XV the Beloved).

Moreover, while there was criticism of the government in France, that had long been compatible with an essentially peaceful politics. This criticism also did not begin in the run-up to Revolution. Instead, various strands of criticism interacted to decry the policies of Louis XIV's last years, of the succeeding Regency government (1715–23), of the ministry of the Duke of Bourbon (1723–26), and of that of Cardinal Fleury (1726–41), especially the clash with the *Parlement* of Paris in 1732. Legal-ecclesiastical disputes over Jansenists and/or Jesuits – disputes which were spread through their schools – continued to be a problem, helping lead to political problems in the 1760s and early 1770s.

At the same time as this continuity, there were changes in the shape of developing notions of nation, public, society and country that were of significance. Indeed, in a major development in political culture, the public mood was increasingly regarded as a source of political legitimacy in the second half of the century. Thus, the notion of honour and *gloire*, generally presented in the seventeenth century in personal (i.e. the monarch) and dynastic terms, was increasingly seen in terms of the nation and country.

Meanwhile, the life of most was very much subject to hardship. Thus, the difficult economic situation in the village of Bilhères in the province of Béarn, a community whose population pressed on its limited food supplies, helped to produce an average age at first marriage of twenty-seven and very few remarriages. The comparable figure between 1774 and 1792 in the Pyrenean village of Azereix was twenty-six and the average gap between births was long, suggesting contraceptive practices. Indeed, the slight decrease in the French birth rate after about 1770 has been attributed in part to the latter, especially *coitus interruptus*, and there are signs that more enlightened priests by then were tacitly allowing contraceptive practices, and that this was affecting the birth rate.

Food scarcity was accompanied by epidemics, for example in Strasbourg until the 1750s. Disease remained a significant killer, but the last major plague epidemic in France occurred in 1720, when a *cordon sanitaire* was successfully imposed to stop the spread from Marseille. Yet, anxiety about plague, including a wrongly identified outbreak of fever in Rouen in 1754, continued. Other diseases remained significant, for example influenza and dysentery, and epidemics of fatal respiratory disease became rife in France during the early 1740s, probably due to hypothermia. The limited nature of the development of medicine, as well as ignorance about hygiene, favoured the spread of epidemics and ensured that remedies were limited. Nevertheless, there was a greater understanding of some of the contributing problems. A royal declaration of 1776 declared that cemeteries in built-up areas that endangered the 'salubrity' of the air must be moved wherever possible, and that only bishops, priests, patrons and seigneurs could be buried inside churches; although there was popular resistance to the attempt to prevent burial inside churches and in Brittany in established *enclos paroissiaux* (parish enclosures).

Due to malnutrition and vitamin shortages, an improved food supply was the most important remedy to disease, as well as being crucial in limiting food riots, which broke out for example in Paris in 1725 and Normandy in 1768. In Paris in the 1750s, seditious comments often cited the high price of bread and the general misery of the people as reasons why Louis XV should be killed. By 1740, public granaries had been built to store food in Besançon, Lyon, Marseille and Strasbourg, but most of the French population was still exposed to grain shortages.

As so often in France, there was regional variation. In Burgundy and Picardy, there was both agricultural improvement and a rise in population, but, in the south-west, major subsistence crises in 1746–48, 1769–72 and 1785–89 helped to weaken the population and to ensure that, during the major epidemics of 1772 and 1787–89, death rates exceeded birth rates. In much of the region, there was no surgeon and the sick had to rely on the priests. Similarly, there was no new demographic regime in Languedoc. In the Pyrenees, there was no sign of an agricultural revolution, the spread of the potato, a new food source, was very slow, and there were regional demographic crises in 1746–47, 1759 and 1769. In the town and hinterland of Ussel in the Massif Central, the economy remained depressed and there was no increase in population as a high rate of infant mortality combined with serious crises of mortality, which produced a high incidence of broken families. The difficulties of improvement were shown in Duravel in Quercy. The cultivation of maize spread there in the first half of the century but, after 1765, the good agricultural lands had been exhausted and, as the limited agricultural techniques did not allow any increase in production by more intensive cultivation, food shortages became a serious problem. In the 1760s, deaths exceeded baptisms and the demographic situation remained poor until the spread of the potato early in the nineteenth century.

Demographic crises had a clear social dimension, which had existed for centuries, but the birth of statistics and the linked attention to social problems permitted a more informed evaluation of the situation. In the poor quarters of Toulouse, birth and death rates were high and many children were abandoned. In contrast, in the wealthier centre of the town, a new and more favourable demographic regime, the so-called demographic transition, developed with lower birth and death rates. Similarly, in Rouen, the mortality rate among the children of the local notables was lower than average, as it also was in villages such as Rosny-sous-Bois near Paris. Doctors were concentrated in the towns and, although France had one doctor for every ten thousand people, in many areas they were a rarity, even if their services could be afforded.

There were numerous signs of social and economic tension, not least as a rising population across much of France forced younger sons and poorer sharecroppers to abandon their hopes of acquiring independent peasant status. As a different, but more poignant, sign of tension, in the 1780s, the average rate of abandonment of children monthly was 160–70 in Lyon and over 650 in Paris. Tragedy, a key feature of life, took its toll. Terrible fires, for example in Rennes in 1720, cattle disease, as in Béarn in 1774, or drought, as in Burgundy in 1778, were exacerbated by limitations in social welfare and insurance that rendered people even more vulnerable. The struggle with wild animals remained an important element, one that it is all too easy to forget, with wolves a serious threat, as near Senlis in 1717 and in the south-west in 1766. In the bad winter of 1783–84, the *Journal de Physique* reported numerous deaths from marauding wolves.

Mysterious animals were also at issue, such as the 'Beast of Gévaudan', possibly a large wolf, in 1764–67. In 1746, Augustin Calmet, a cleric and scholar, published a book on vampires, only for the belief to be attacked in the *Encyclopédie* in 1765 and by Voltaire in 1772, but popular attitudes were more supportive. Moreover, in Paris, in 1749–50, it was widely believed that children were being seized and killed in order to provide blood for baths to help Louis XV combat leprosy, which was a pointed reversal of the idea of the monarch as a sacred healer. More generally, and notably in rural areas, there was a sense of factors over which control was limited, while, on a long-established pattern that may throw light on prehistoric cave paintings, this was an animistic world inhabited by spirits, with death no necessary barrier. In his biography of his father, *La vie de mon père* (1778), Nicolas Restif de la Bretonne (1734–1806) recorded that in his paternal milieu, that of a wealthy peasant near Auxerre, shepherds told tales of the transmigration of souls to animals and werewolves. In 1727, Cardinal Fleury, the leading minister, expressed his belief that the Devil was able to thrash his human subjects.

In this context, the Church appeared to offer a form of necessary white magic and, in 1725, when Paris was threatened with flooding and a bad harvest, the reliquary of the local patron saint, Geneviève, was carried in procession in the hope of stopping the heavy rain, as in 1696 it had been deployed against drought. In 1775, church bells in Dijon were rung to drive away a storm, while in 1788 a violent gale on the north-west coast was met by solemn processions to the churches and night-time services. Meanwhile, despite opposition, the peasants of Bresse persisted in their celebration of Midsummer's Night, combining the Catholic liturgy with pagan customs. Yet de-Christianization had already begun in the Paris region in the mid-century.

The seriousness of bad weather was increased because agriculture was the key sector of the economy. In 1789, 74 per cent of the active population – a fairly typical figure – in the Vivarais region was employed in agriculture, while many of those who worked in rural industry, as in French Flanders, also tended plots of land or were members of a family economy in which another member was a part of the agricultural workforce. Moreover, industry was often closely linked to the agricultural hinterland, as with the town of Niort, where animal skins played an important role in the 1720s and which depended on receiving large numbers of those of goat kids. It was not surprising that the economic writers of mid-century, known as the 'physiocrats' – Quesnay, Dupont de Nemours, Mirabeau and Mercier de La Rivière – argued that the increase in wealth in the manufacturing and commercial spheres could only take place on the basis of prior increases in the amount of raw materials extracted from nature. They claimed that the land was the sole source of real wealth, that manufacturing simply changed the form of its products, and that trade only moved them. The physiocratic call for more investment in agriculture was combined with proposals designed to increase its profitability. The argument that grain must be allowed to rise to its natural price level and that, to that end, restrictions on its sale, such as export prohibitions, should be reduced, was intended to transfer more of the benefit of grain production to the rural community, notably the peasantry.

Although there was no agricultural revolution to match England, with its emphasis on leguminous crops and enclosure, there was an attempt to clear waste ground so as to expand cultivation and to improve techniques. In 1759, the Academy of Besançon organized a competition for the discovery of a vegetable substance capable of replacing bread in case of need, and it was won by the young Antoine Parmentier, the popularizer in France of the potato. Maize was more popular in the south-west, playing a major role in helping the large growth of population. France was largely split along the forty-fifth parallel, with the potato crucial to the north and maize to the south, although maize was also crucial in the Loire Valley in the north.

Long-distance trades linked distant regions. Lean cattle were driven for fattening from Auvergne to lush lower Normandy, before they were moved to the Parisian market. Orléans's economy benefited from the transhipment of Languedoc and Anjou wine for movement to the markets of Paris and Rouen. Wine, olive oil and fruit from the south were moved up the Rhône to Lyon, and thence by land to Roanne and by boat along the Loire, Canal de Briare, Canal du Loing and Seine to Paris. These long-distance trades created opportunities for local markets and developed local production, while, overlapping this, there was activity for local markets in the shape of satisfying local demand. Thus, Languedoc wine production developed thanks to the growth of the provincial market.

There were, however, many problems. Improved agricultural methods spread unevenly, and a scarcity of livestock in the north was matched by a lack of fodder, which ensured that weak animals pulled the poorly constructed ploughs, producing an inadequate seedbed. There were also social problems. For example, in the Loire Valley, small peasant holdings were acquired by bourgeois and noble landholders, whose grain-growing and cattle-raising estates, farmed by *métayers* (sharecroppers), were not character-ized by improved farming methods.

In France, there was industry, but no Industrial Revolution and relatively few large-scale industrial units. Much of the industry was in rural areas and, in 1779, the government gave in to merchant pressure and relaxed restrictions on the rural production of cloth. As a consequence, greater quantities of lower-quality cloth were produced by relatively unskilled rural workers, while wages and prices were kept low. In Picardy in the 1780s, thousands of looms in the wool, linen and hosiery industries were supplied with yarn by the spinning of peasant women. Mechanization did not move at the pace of Britain, although, in 1784, the framework knitters of lower Champagne began to make use of cotton yarn spun *à la mécanique*, and the mechanization of cotton spinning also began in the Norman town of Louviers.

The diversity of circumstances and the varied social dynamics of industrialization were important to the pattern of French life then and thereafter, notably in the nineteenth century. For example, although Toulouse had a cloth industry, it was not a major industrial and commercial city, while Marseille contained cloth, sugar, glass, porcelain and soap factories. The contrast in their industrial structure owed much to their differing roles as trading centres. In Troyes, where a large portion of the working population was employed in the cotton industry, raw cotton was imported from the West Indies and cotton cloth exported to Italy, Spain and southern France, the industry being run by merchants, not clothiers. A very different account can be offered if it is noted that the 1780s were the peak decade for the receipt of slaves shipped from Africa by the West Indian colonies, notably Saint-Domingue (Haiti). This was an important aspect of France's Atlantic economy, with Saint-Domingue in particular a major producer of sugar and coffee. Bordeaux, Nantes, Le Havre and La Rochelle benefited in particular.

There was also variety alongside improvement in communications, with the transportation network substantially denser and more interconnected north of a line stretching from Geneva to Saint-Malo than south of it. There was no integrated national framework, although there was a substantial improvement in the road system after 1750, particularly in Languedoc, and journey times were reduced. The École des Ponts et Chaussées (School of Bridges and Roads), established in Paris in 1747, was partly responsible for the development of bridge building, but road construction usually followed existing routes, as in Languedoc. In 1775, Louis XVI (r. 1774–1792) had to alter his plans for touching for scrofula in Champagne (which he did, reviving a practice last held in 1738) because the roads were impracticable and the passage of the rivers uncertain. Hot-air balloons, first manned in 1783, rose to 6,000 feet, but their steering was perfunctory, and there were no significant consequences from this innovation. The self-educated Joseph Montgolfier also focused his ideas on the expansive power of heat and worked on a heat pump, an ancestor of the internal combustion engine.

As a more lasting constant, the failings of the financial system were dramatically demonstrated in 1720 with the collapse of the fiscal system. The Duke of Orléans authorized a Scot, John Law, to establish a private bank in 1716. Law believed in the demonetization of coinage and its replacement by paper credit. Arguing that the circulation of money was a source of wealth, Law was a supporter of an expansionary monetary policy that would lower interest rates, with banknotes serving to stimulate the economy, especially agriculture, in which resources were underutilized. Increased circulation of money would thus, he hoped, improve the income of community and king. Orléans's support allowed Law to implement some of his plans. In 1717, he founded the Mississippi Company to exploit the economic potential believed to be present in the new colony of Louisiana. In 1718, his bank became the state one, but it proved inadequate to the burden and collapsed in a spectacular fashion.

The deployment of the use of reason in intellectual life included the debate over how best to govern the kingdom, while history was used as the source and evidence of the right approach. In his *Histoire critique de l'établissement de la monarchie française dans les Gaules* (1734), the Abbé Jean-Baptiste Dubos (1670–1742) argued that the royal authority of the Bourbons represented a rightful return to the situation under the Franks in the eighth and ninth centuries. Dubos presented this as a return, after a long period of usurpation in which the aristocracy had been too powerful, indeed acting as usurpers of rightful royal authority. For Dubos, the authority of Clovis derived from that of the Roman emperors, which was an apparently appropriate, albeit inaccurate, account of legitimacy.

On a pattern that was in part a reaction against Louis XIV, this positive argument toward royal authority clashed with that, advanced by the Count of Boulainvilliers (1658–1722), of the nobility as playing a key limiting role because they were descended from freedom-loving Franks who had conquered those weakened by imperial rule, in other words overthrowing the foreign control of Rome over what, with this conquest, became France. Moreover, Boulainvilliers, author of the posthumously published *Histoire de l'ancien gouvernement de la France* (1727), claimed that Clovis had been elected by the other Franks, thus implying that consent was a key element in subsequent legitimacy. In his *L'esprit des lois* (1748), Charles-Louis, Baron of Montesquieu (1689–1755), answered Dubos by stressing the need to keep despotism at a distance, which was very much the theme of his constitutional speculation. These historical tensions and themes played a role in the attitude of the nobility toward the Crown in the early stages of the Revolution.

Meanwhile, François-Marie Arouet, alias Voltaire (1694–1778), the most prominent *philosophe*, wrote a series of histories criticizing past authoritarianism, notably in *La Ligue* (1723), later renamed *La Henriade*, and *Le Siècle de Louis XIV* (1751), which condemned Louis's concern with *gloire*. In his *Essai sur les moeurs et l'esprit des nations* (1745–53), Voltaire wrote a world history within a universal context rather than within a Christian or nationalist framework. History attracted what was more generally seen as an enlightened approach.

If new attitudes were affecting the political culture, earlier in the century there had already been comparable criticism without this leading to revolution. Serious defeat by Britain and Prussia in the Seven Years War (1756–63) had been prefigured in the War of the Spanish Succession (1701–14), and there had long been fiscal strains and political criticism. If the names of ministers such as Maupeou, Vergennes and Calonne, rather than the monarchs, played a major role in the discussion of eighteenth-century governmental action and politics, that was not a new departure as it had also been the case with Richelieu and Mazarin. The character and attitudes of individual monarchs were important, but so were the ministerial politics that joined the development of hierarchies of policy-making and administration, and clashes over policy, to more entrenched issues of patronage. Nevertheless, the contrast between the official rhetoric of authority and triumph, and the reality of limited power, was less significant for the seventeenth century, than during the Enlightenment, when the potential of government to improve public welfare was more clearly understood. As a result, the expectations placed upon ministers and their accountability were increased in what became the prelude to the Revolution. Then, thinkers increasingly grasped the potential of government, especially as a means to mobilize the resources of society so as to maximize the public welfare. Thomas Pelham noted when he visited Lyon in 1777:

> there is a plan in agitation and indeed began for turning the course of the Rhône so as to prevent the junction of the Saône till at a league below the town: to make several additional streets with a large square; and a channel to run between the two rivers and supplied by them both, on which they propose making corn mills in order to avoid the present incommodious method of having mills on boats in the river.

Such schemes could be fruitless, but they provided an instance of the sense of capacity for change. Demands for more, and more readily accessible and useable, information included the national enquiry to identify and assess mineral resources ordered by the Regent in 1716. Economic policy continued to attract attention. Free-market economics, notably deregulation rather than the usual nostrums of state action, was to be stressed by Jacques-Claude Vincent de Gournay, an intendant of commerce in 1751–59 who coined the term 'bureaucracy', government of desks, and Étienne Bonnot de Condillac in his *Le commerce et le gouvernement* (1776).

Information was also important for scientific reasons, as with the expeditions sent to Lapland and Ecuador in 1735 in order to test the sphericity of the Earth. Pierre de Maupertuis (1698–1759), the mathematician who went to Lapland, told the story as an heroic instance of scientific endeavour. Voltaire commented of his book, 'In ecstasy and in fear, I follow you…up your mountains of ice.' Like the other *philosophes*, Maupertuis's writings straddled the divide between hard science and populism, and works such as

Vénus physique, in which he considered the origins of life, reflected his keen sense of wider, public interest.

Important writers offered a degree of cultural relativism that challenged the role of religion. In 1721, Usbek and Rica, the two Persian (Iranian) visitors to the West in Montesquieu's influential *Lettres persanes*, commented on Pope Clement XI as a 'conjurer who makes people believe that three [God, Jesus and the Holy Spirit] are only one; that wine is not wine and bread not bread', a sweeping attack on transubstantiation. Denis Diderot, the editor of the *Encyclopédie*, in his *Supplément au voyage de Bougainville*, a work written in 1772 but only published in 1796, used the Pacific, as revealed in Bougainville's visit to Tahiti in 1768, to attack Western morality and religion. Geological research, such as that of Jean-Étienne Guettard in 1751 in the Puy de Dôme, threw doubt on the biblical view of the age of the Earth.

Launched in Paris in 1751, the *Encyclopédie*, originally a project to translate and enlarge an English work, became in practice a vehicle for propaganda for the ideas of the *philosophes*, and, in his article 'Encyclopédie', Diderot wrote that, by helping people to become better informed, such a work would assist them to become more virtuous and happier. A guide to the known, the *Encyclopédie* discarded speculation about the unknown, a focus that encouraged a sense of human achievement, and distanced the work from the occult and the mystical. Published in French, not Latin, and produced by subscription and individual support, and not by government commission, the *Encyclopédie* testified to the public, commercial character of culture.

Usefulness was not only a key theme of the *Encyclopédie*. Georges-Louis Leclerc, Count Buffon, the influential director of the Jardin du Roi in Paris, published a thirty-six-volume *Histoire naturelle* (1749–89) that achieved great popularity and fame, and, testifying to the fashion for encyclopaedic knowledge, offered a taxonomic classification. It reflected Buffon's view that information was a means to enable humanity to fulfil its potential, with reform presented as dependent on the rational governance of nature in order to improve the economy and enhance the human environment. Buffon also experimented, notably with cross breeding.

Antoine Lavoisier (1743–1794) provided a major scientific contribution that exemplified the particular French inflection of acquiring more information through experimentation and advancing new ideas of classification. Through his experiments, he came to the conclusion that the weight of all compounds obtained by chemical reaction is equal to that of the reacting substances, a conclusion that he generalized as the law of conservation of mass in 1789, while his *Méthode de nomenclature chimique* (1787) defined a system of quantification that could be used to facilitate comparative experimentation. Lavoisier systemized the chemistry of gases in his *Traité élémentaire de chimie* (1789) and the methodology of chemistry was now very different to alchemy. The *philosophes* applauded science as an example of human creativity, emphasizing experimentation over *a priori* systematization, as in Étienne Bonnot de Condillac's *Traité des systèmes* (1749); meanwhile, the public tributes of the Académie des Sciences helped to establish an image of scientists as dispassionate seekers after truth.

As ever, it is too easy to leave religion out of the account, but it was significant across a range of spheres, including the arts where it is not commonly to the fore in discussion of this period. Thus, Neoclassicism became increasingly important in Paris, as with Nicolas Nicole's church of the Madeleine (built 1746–66) and Jacques-Germain Soufflot's church of Sainte Geneviève, now the Panthéon (1758–90). The primacy of the Classical 'look' in the second half of the century led to the altering of many Gothic churches, by giving the bases and capitals of pillars a Classical appearance and by removing Gothic ornamentation judged hideous, such as the altars, rood screens and choir stalls of Saint-Germain l'Auxerrois in 1756. Churches were often whitewashed and stained glass was removed.

More generally, alongside criticism of the Church, as well as what some later scholars have referred to as de-Christianization, there was much sign of traditional practice and belief. For example, in northern Alsace, pilgrimages and old cults, such as that of Sainte Odile, the patroness of the region, continued; a populace that was far from de-Christianized was served by a clergy that had little interest in Enlightenment ideas. This was true also in Brittany, with many chapels dedicated to early Celtic saints unrecognized by the official Catholic calendar. Semi-legendary saints such as Noyale, Tréphine and Trémeur were believed to have been beheaded by pagans and to have either carried their head to their chosen interment site or had it restored by saints such as Gildas. Every year, large processions took place to such chapels in the ritual (which persists today) of the Pardon. A time for repentance and prayer, and afterwards for feasting and dancing, the Pardon remained deeply anchored in popular piety. Popular culture continued its long and varied interaction with Christianity, more successfully so than the attempt in the 1790s to create a religion from the utopianism of the French Revolution.

In 1759, the *Parlement* of Paris was informed by the Attorney General, Joly de Fleury, that there existed 'a society organized... to propagate material, to destroy religion, to inspire a spirit of independence and to nourish the corruption of morals'. This was blamed on works such as the *Encyclopédie*. However, a striking feature of the writings of most Enlightenment figures was their ability to reconcile their theoretically subversive notions of reason with the suppositions of traditional authority, so that challenges to Christian teachings, as opposed to Christian teachers, were few.

The crusading zeal of particular Enlightenment campaigns, for example against torture and against the Jesuits, was not matched by a consistent programme, other than one expressed in generalities, such as tolerance and reason.

Defined as a fashion and a clique, the Enlightenment and the *philosophes* reached their peak in the 1760s. Their pretensions offended many, the young Genevan academic Horace Benedict de Saussure writing in 1768 of Jean-François Marmontel, a leading contributor to the *Encyclopédie*'s articles about literature:

> I recognized in him what I had been warned to expect in Parisian *beaux esprits* – a very arbitrary tone, a habit of speaking of his set as the only one to be called philosophic, and of despising and making odious insinuations against those who did not belong to it.

Indeed, the Enlightenment was an attitude, rather than a movement with a programme. New trends were apparent from the 1770s, especially the pre-Romanticism that appeared to reject balance, but they were less a stark challenge to the Enlightenment than the product of the diverse and often incompatible ideas of the period, ideas that had been given a false coherence by the cult of reason. There was nothing inevitable about these ideas leading to revolution by the end of the century.

8. The Revolution, 1789–1799

July 1789 was not a peaceful time for British tourists in Paris, as Samuel Boddington noted:

> The heads of the Governor and Commandant of the Bastille just cut off from their bodies carrying in triumph….In the evening it was rumoured about the City that the Duc D'Artois, the King's Brother [later Charles X] was within a few miles of the City with 30,000 men and to make an assault upon it that night…the sound of all the bells of the City calling to arms, drums beating and cannon drawing about – the pavement before our hotel taking up and carried to the top of the opposite house to throw upon the soldiers in case of an assault, together with the impression made on our minds by the sights we had just seen, all tended to have an effect upon us which was not of the most agreeable kind.

Lord Henry Fitzroy observed the celebrations at the Champ de Mars for the first anniversary of the fall of the Bastille in 1790:

> History never did before nor probably never will again give a description of so many people assembled together….The Champ of Mars about 2 miles round was like a large amphitheatre with benches of about 50 rows in breadth all round….In the centre was an altar of a considerable height …their deputies took the oath, immediately after La Fayette, as a representative of

the whole people ascended aloft upon the altar, and there took the oath in the name of the people amidst the hues and cries of the whole mob and uplifting of the swords of the deputies and guards. *Innumerable* cannons were fired close to the place during the whole fete….The King was expected to have descended from his throne and taken the oath at the altar, but did not, which seems to have given great offence to many people, and I dread the consequences.

These two moments encapsulate the sense of tragedy and triumph that engulfed France in the late eighteenth century. The lasting consequences of the Revolution, its success in creating a new constitutional, political, ideological and religious order, in defeating domestic and foreign opponents, and in bringing change to other states, were of fundamental importance in French and European history and remain of great significance today, for France's identity was never to be the same again. That, however, does not necessarily make the origins of the Revolution of comparable importance and uniqueness, and it was not surprising that nearly all German newspapers devoted more space in 1789 to the Austro-Turkish War than to events in France. Indeed, many of the problems affecting France in the late 1780s were far from novel. Earlier crises in eighteenth-century France also entailed appeals to public opinion, as well as ministerial instability, court faction and unpredictable outcomes. Earlier in the century, the classic ministerial techniques of negotiation, bluff and raising the stakes could also swiftly convert confrontation into crisis, and royal brinkmanship had always risked a slide into ever deeper problems.

The collapse of the political regime in the summer of 1789 can therefore be explained in traditional terms; but that was not true of what replaced it, and, in one light, the escalation of domestic political conflict in 1789 was out of proportion to the gravity of the issues. The causes and origins of the Revolution have long been a source of major debate, at once academic and political. The Musée de la Révolution française in Vizille, where the Estates of Dauphiné met on 21 July 1788 after the riot in Grenoble of the *Journée des Tuiles* (Day of the Tiles, 7 June), offers a perspective that is not metropolitan, which is a valuable qualification to the frequent partisanship of the debate. Historians on the Left were, and still to a degree are, apt to see the struggle in class terms, and with reference to Marxist ideas. But, in 1789, Paris and other cities still had very few factories, and the Revolutionary movements were not the achievement of factory workers, although the Réveillon riots in Paris that April centred on a small factory and were an important harbinger of later large-scale popular movements in the capital. Only in Paris's northern suburbs were there a few large textile manufactories employing between 400 and 800 workers, and one-third of Parisian workers were employed in the traditional building trade. Moreover, rather than simply stressing factors for change, there were backward-looking aspects to the economic dimension of the Revolution, so that the guilds in the cloth-making city of Troyes both demanded the suppression of rural manufacturing and attacked the use of the spinning jenny for causing unemployment.

There was rural disaffection in France, leading to the paranoid attacks on landlords in the *grande peur* (great fear) of 1789, but such peasant violence was not new, nor unique to France. Indeed, the idea that class tension explains the Revolution is deeply problematic. The current tendency among British historians, instead, is to focus on political factors, especially short-term ones, and these factors were certainly crucial in the early stages. Revisionist interpretations that play down the existence of social tension and stress, instead, the radicalizing role of the very collapse of political authority tend both to adopt a narrative rather than theoretical approach, one focusing both on political action and divisions, and on the role of chance, and to emphasize the extent and impact of Revolutionary disruption and violence. In recent years, there has also been a great deal of attention paid to questions of political culture that go far beyond the political narrative, with work on representation, symbolism and violence, which, in turn, has affected how we see 'extreme' and 'moderate' Revolutionaries.

Religious factors do not tend to play a role in the discussion of the causes of the Revolution, but there was a relationship between the weakness of the indoctrinating institutions and practices of the Counter-Reformation, indeed the dismantling of them in the case of the suppression of the Jesuits (in France in 1762), and the multiple ideological tensions of Catholic Europe in the 1780s. A lessened emphasis on the sacral aspect of kingship encouraged a stress on the monarch as the first servant of the state, which was an aspect both of a spread of reform Catholicism that owed something to Jansenism, and of a more general process of the social and cultural transformation of established hierarchies that was particularly evident in government aspirations and in major cities such as Paris.

The political impetus for constitutional redefinitions and innovations came largely from the government. In the 1770s and 1780s, struggling to cope with the debt caused by intervention in the American War of Independence, French ministries sought to create a consensus similar to that offered by the British Parliament, trying to ground French government in institutions that were representative of public opinion, by planning provincial assemblies, and then summoning, first, an Assembly of Notables (1787) and, subsequently, in accordance with pressure from the latter, the Estates-General (1789). By the end of 1787, political opposition ensured that the streamlined 'Absolutist' monarchy was no longer an option, and economic and fiscal problems meant that a multi-layered crisis developed: of the economy, of state finance and credit-worthiness, and of the very process of government. Possibly no acceptable solution could have been devised as it was difficult to take those who had little, or any, experience of the problems of central government into either confidence or a limited degree of partnership, and to persuade them to employ their newfound role in coping with difficult circumstances. It was far easier for them to press demands for greater power, and to voice the suspicions and fears that arose from the divided court, unstable ministries and rapidly changing policies of the period; although none of these characteristics was new.

The attempted transition to a newly revived representative character in France's constitutional monarchy was difficult, in part because of Louis XVI's unwillingness to be flexible, but the failure was far from inevitable. Related to this, but also separate, the Revolution was far from a homogeneous and linear process, but, instead, developed in fits and starts. The lack of international prestige after the successful assistance in 1778–83 to the American Revolution was a notable factor, and total failure in the Dutch Crisis of 1787 was important. The contrast in October 1789 between the delirious celebrations with which the Viennese greeted the news of the Austrian capture of Belgrade from the Turks, and the forced transfer of Louis XVI and the Court from Versailles to Paris after the invasion of the palace on 6 October, is a pointed reminder of the political value of success and the way in which it was easier to obtain through military victory than through internal policies.

Louis was not helped by his inability to manage court factions, including difficulties with his brothers and his cousin, the radical Louis Philippe, Duke of Orléans (who became known as 'Philippe Égalité'), who helped to undermine Louis's position and was eventually to vote for his execution, only to fall victim himself to the Terror and be guillotined in November 1793. From the other extreme, one of Louis's brothers, the Count of Artois, later Charles X, opposed any diminution of monarchical authority. The divisions in the royal family weakened the court, a traditional theme.

The monarchy, moreover, had been tarnished by a series of scandals, especially the involvement of the immature Queen Marie Antoinette, in the fraudulent Diamond Necklace Affair of 1785–86. The lack of respect for the monarch took pornographic form, especially in accounts, true or fictional, of the loves of Louis XV and Marie Antoinette, both of which hit the reputation of the royal family. More generally, scandals became public topics as tales of marital betrayal and breakdown became infused with political meaning. This lack of respect was to culminate in the trial and execution of Louis XVI in 1792–93: monarchy apparently was invalid because the monarch lacked the attributes of leadership. Earlier French anticipations of unimpressive kingship did not lessen the problems created in an age of personal monarchy by Louis XV's failure, in his last two decades, to maintain royal *gloire* and by Louis XVI's pedestrian lack of appeal. He failed to win personal glory on the battlefield, seriously lacked charisma, and was unable either to control the tempo of or exert control over domestic affairs. Louis XVI, moreover, failed to use the court to develop his *gloire* and to strengthen his relations with the aristocracy.

A new aesthetic of public, even republican, dedication was also significant, one most clearly expressed in the virtuous Neoclassicism of Jacques-Louis David's paintings, notably *Le Serment des Horaces* (*The Oath of the Horatii*, 1784, see pl. VIII). There were related scientific developments that were similarly designed to present integrity, with the development of descriptive geometry between 1768 and 1780 by the mathematician Gaspard Monge enabling mathematically rigorous graphical presentation. Such rigour was linked to a Neoclassical style of precision in which the abstract value of mathematics played an aesthetic as well as an intellectual role. The Marquis de Condorcet pressed, in the *Essai sur l'application de l'analyse à la probabilité des décisions rendues à la pluralité des voix* (1785), for the use of probability in order to enable people to make rational decisions instead of relying on instinct and passion. A great believer in the possibility of indefinite progress through human action, he saw the key in universal state education focused on practical subjects. Like Lavoisier, who was arrested in 1793 and executed in 1794, Condorcet was to be a victim of the Revolution of which he had been an active supporter, serving as secretary of the Legislative Assembly and backing female suffrage, only to be arrested by the Jacobins in 1794, dying in prison soon after. The Jacobins, who took their name from their regular meeting place, a Jacobin convent, were a powerful group of Revolutionary egalitarians known for their radicalism and ruthlessness in the years that followed 1789, and their support of the Terror.

Called to try to resolve the politico-fiscal crisis, the elections to the Estates-General early in 1789 increased political participation, tension and expectations. In each electoral district, the three estates or orders (clergy, nobles and commoners, meaning the middle class) separately drew up *cahiers de doléances*, lists of grievances that they wanted redressed, in part to clarify the constitutional nature of the monarchy and its relationship with the legal rights of its subjects. Guaranteed rights, representative government, a reformed church and taxation only by consent were clear demands; and the political pivot of the new order was to be the powers of an Estates-General and of provincial Estates, all of which were to meet regularly. Decentralization was a key demand but, at this stage, radicalism was limited. Separation of powers, not republicanism, was sought, and there was little interest in the abolition of the nobility, of monasticism, of urban and provincial privileges, and of tithes.

Nevertheless, the content of the *cahiers* was less important than their existence, and, from a financial crisis, the entire governmental and political structure was now called into question. The Estates-General was expected to reform the state in conjunction with the monarchy, and the elections and the *cahiers* created new links between an emerging public political world in the localities and the metropolitan arena of national politics. The king was not regarded as a problem in the *cahiers*, indeed he was seen as popular in many peasant ones. Local deliberations on national political concerns took place against a collapse in many areas of government authority with serious economic difficulties playing a major role in the breakdown of order in many towns and in much of the countryside.

As a result of demands at the time of the *Fronde* being thwarted, the Estates-General had last met in 1614, and, when it convened at Versailles on 5 May 1789, it reflected the distribution of political power in France. The Third Estate, the commoners, included no peasant or artisan representatives. There were hopes of creating a new political understanding but, lacking political skill, Louis XVI proved unwilling to work effectively with those supporting reform. Indeed, the Estates-General became not only a forum for national politics, but also a body before which the government was crippled. The pace of political reform, the urgent desire to create a new constitution and, crucially, the opposition of powerful domestic elements to the process of reform and bitter divisions among those who sought change ensured that the desire for reform soon became better described as revolution. Heady oratory, pressure of circumstances and a growing sense of crisis led the Third Estate on 17 June 1789 to declare themselves the National Assembly and to claim a measure of sovereignty as the only elected representatives of the people. The government countered by planning a 'Royal Session' to reassert Louis's authority.

The preparatory prohibition of any meetings by the Estates, however, led the angry deputies, wrongly concluding that a dissolution was intended, to assemble on 20 June in an indoor tennis court and, in an atmosphere of heightened emotion, to pledge themselves not to disperse until reform was complete and the constitution of France was clarified.

Eventually held on 23 June, the Royal Session was a failure. Support for the king was ebbing, his preferred reforms were too late, and the Third Estate refused to disperse. Louis backed down, while public order collapsed in Paris. On 27 June, Louis, now vulnerable, told the clergy and nobles to join the National Assembly. Political crisis, meanwhile, coincided with a food shortage, and Britain rejected a French request for grain supplies. Peasants refused to pay seigneurial dues and tithes, and began to attack châteaux. As the price of grain peaked in Paris, the Bastille prison was seized on 14 July in an outburst of popular and violent action.

Plans for a royalist counter-revolution in Paris were thwarted, in part due to a lack of confidence about the position of the army. The troops lived among the population, pursuing civilian trades when not on duty, and were thus subject to the economic and ideological pressures affecting the people. The pressure for change was now apparently too great to stop. The National Assembly created, on 28 July, committees of reports and research that permitted it to supervise administrative affairs and to pursue those suspected of subversion against the new regime. On 4 August, it followed this by abolishing all feudal rights and dues. Moreover, its 26 August 'Declaration of the Rights of Man and the Citizen' claimed that men were free and equal in rights and that the purpose of all political association was to preserve the rights of man. Louis's reluctance to accept reform, including his reluctance to assent to the Declaration of the Rights of Man and the Citizen, focused uncertainty and mistrust, resulting, in a Paris still affected by bread shortages, to the 'October Days'. Rumours of preparations for a counter-revolution led a Parisian crowd, including many women, to march on 5 October 1789 on Versailles, determined to bring Louis to Paris. After the queen's apartments were stormed by a section of the crowd on the 6th, the king, under pressure, went to the Tuileries Palace in Paris. With Versailles abandoned and the volatile metropolis ever more the centre of politics, royal authority and power were exploded. As yet, however, there was no solid alternative. The rapid speed of changes, and the absence of sufficient time, trust and shared views to permit the development of stable constitutional conventions and techniques of parliamentary management, helped to keep the relationship between the royal government and the National Assembly unsettled, but so did differences over policy. Above all, there was a crucial lack of trust, and on both sides. But for this, a new-model constitutional monarchy could have worked.

In 1790, itself a largely peaceful year, royal powers were eroded, while differences over the working of a constitutional monarchy focused on the Church. Its property was nationalized and it turned into a branch of the civil service. The National Assembly imposed an oath on the clergy to support the new order, with dismissal as the penalty for refusal, a divisive step that helped undermine support for the Revolution in many parts of France. Moreover, the abolition of nobility in 1790 left the monarchy vulnerable as traditional respect for rank was attacked.

Radical ideas, meanwhile, spread as a consequence of the developing crisis. This spread owed much to the extent to which there was a clear social character to many of the factional alignments. The conservative groups were dominated by the privileged; and socio-cultural divisions among the deputies, especially between the nobility and the bourgeoisie, helped to focus and sustain political perceptions. Thus, alongside the title of the Paris newspaper

Postillon extraordinaire, in June 1790, was the declaration: 'No more Princes, No more Dukes, No more Counts, No more Masters.' There was enthusiasm in a number of regions for the first anniversary of the fall of the Bastille. One of the foremost centres of enthusiasm was the town of Pontivy in the heart of Brittany, which hosted a meeting of the Breton-Angevin Federation in which its members renounced all particular privileges and local loyalties: as citizens of France, they would resist all attempts to take away their natural human rights. The army, the bourgeois and even peasants and the clergy crowded the town to celebrate the oath. Such views were increasingly expressed but, at this stage, there was no strong radical ideological drive, and it is possible that a constitutional monarchy would have been viable if Louis and the conservative aristocracy had been willing to support it.

The political crisis of the Revolution had, however, transformed the army. The majority of officers fled France, while there were serious mutinies, notably at Nancy in 1790, as well as the breakdown of discipline. Long-established links and hierarchies were put aside; for example, in 1791, the names traditionally used for regiments were replaced by numbers. After the initial heady enthusiasm of some, tourists found the situation troubling, and more avoided Paris. Carriages were stopped by the National Guard, and there was growing antagonism towards foreigners.

Increasingly concerned that his position was unsustainable, Louis decided to flee to the safety of a frontier fortress and then pursue a negotiated restoration of his authority. However, on 21 June 1791, while doing so, he was recognized en route to Montmédy, stopped by a crowd at Varennes, and returned to Paris. The problem of a monarch out of sympathy with developments in his country was now very public and led to rising support for republicanism, which increased in April 1792 when war was declared on Austria. To the Revolutionaries, it appeared crucial to mobilize mass support for a struggle with an insidious, but all too apparent, enemy: an obvious foreign rival supporting domestic conspiracy and insurrection. Paranoia drove a rapidly developing language of nationalism, with revolution and radicalization the cause and consequence of this process of struggle.

Creating the concept of a sovereign will of the Revolutionary people, to which all opposition was illegitimate, encouraged this fervour, as did serious initial failures in the war. On 10 August 1792, the radicals took power, with the Tuileries Palace stormed and Louis seized, while the monarchy was suspended by the Legislative Assembly; and, in the place of both, a National Convention, theoretically elected by universal male suffrage, was established in September. With the establishment of a republic, popular sovereignty was thrust to the fore. Foreign diplomats had been accredited to Louis, and the collapse of his government led to a break in formal relations. September also saw the massacre of those held in the Parisian prisons, many of them arrested on suspicion of treasonable activities, and rapidly sentenced to death as an aspect of 'people's justice'. The September Massacres, of 1,100 to 1,400 people including over 200 priests, helped to unite much European opinion against the Revolution, and atrocity literature circulated widely.

The Prussian advance on Paris, however, was blocked by larger French forces at Valmy on 20 September and, in a swift change of fortune, by the end of November, Savoy, the Austrian Netherlands (Belgium) and much of the Rhineland had been overrun by French armies, a victory over the Austrians at Jemappes in Belgium on 6 November being crucial. On 19 November, the National Convention passed a decree declaring that the French people would extend fraternity and assistance to all peoples seeking to regain their liberty, a principle that was subversive of all international order. Eight days later, Savoy, conquered from the kingdom of

Sardinia, was incorporated into France. Montbéliard, which followed in 1793, has remained French since. Alongside the rhetoric of internationalism, the outbreak of war turned the Revolution towards an increasingly nationalistic tone and focus.

The pace and pressure of frenetic change did not abate. On 3 December 1792, the decision was taken to try Louis, while, on 15 December, a decree to ensure that the *ancien régime* be swept away in territories occupied by French forces was promulgated: elections were to be held to create a new order, but the electorate was restricted to adult men ready to swear an oath to be 'faithful to the people and the principles of liberty and equality'. It was anticipated that people thus 'freed' would support and seek 'union' with France. On 21 January 1793, Louis was guillotined in the Place de la Révolution (now the Place de la Concorde). Britain, the Netherlands and Spain soon after joined the coalition of Austria and Prussia against France.

As the Revolutionary regime struggled with a growing range of foreign foes, it became increasingly radical. The Girondins, a group that dominated both the Jacobin Club and the government in 1792, successfully pressing for war with Austria, were overthrown by their opponents, the Montagnards, who were more radical (although in their advocacy of war to save their political skins, the Girondins can be seen as irresponsibly extreme). The Paris National Guard purged the Girondins in a coup of 31 May–2 June 1793, while, using the Revolutionary Tribunal established in March and the Committee of Public Safety in April, which Maximilien Robespierre (1758–1794) joined in July, the Montagnards launched a fully fledged Terror in July. The regime denounced all obstacles as the work of nefarious 'enemies of the Revolution'. Robespierre, a lawyer who was a member of the Jacobin Club, had been a notable agitator in the lead up to the Revolution, and now he became the principal architect of the

Terror directed against both its opponents and even its moderate supporters.

The Terror was radical, both in its objectives and in its lower-class connotations. Nevertheless, the cause of the people was employed to keep them in order. Indeed, the people were not trusted. Between the creation of the National Convention in September 1792 and its dissolution in the autumn of 1795, no legislative elections took place; only at the local level were a few assemblies convened for municipal and judicial purposes. Apart from the abortive constitution of 1793, the Convention was not prepared to let the people have a direct say in whom they elected as their deputies. Elections offered the possibility of democracy, but the elites thwarted this process with a two-tier procedure intended to filter out popular elements. Moreover, the press was curbed. The legislation issued by the Revolutionary governments brought no real improvement for the poor because the country lacked the wealth and tax base to support an effective and generous national welfare system. Without economic growth, the secular philosophies of change and improvement were flawed, and it is not surprising that most radical thinkers were sceptical about the appeal of their views to the bulk of the population. Whatever their stated belief in the sovereignty of the people might be, they were hostile to what they viewed as popular superstition and conservatism. In 1793, Louis de Saint-Just, a prominent member of the Committee of Public Safety, later called the 'Angel of Death', stated that 'men must be made what they should be'. It is not surprising that their imposed public virtue had only limited appeal. Besides being impractical, it was largely irrelevant to the problems of most people.

Summary justice led in the Terror to the death of many royalists as well as those Revolutionaries seen as insufficiently radical, including the Girondins and rival Jacobins, notably Georges

Danton (1759–1794) and the extreme Jacques Hébert. Danton had been a pivotal figure in the early days of the Revolution, but he often disagreed with Robespierre and pleaded for an end to the Terror. He was charged with conspiracy and corruption and, on 5 April 1794, led to the guillotine. The Revolutionary courts passed 16,594 death sentences, although many others died in prison or without trial. Paris and Nantes were particular centres of Revolutionary slaughter. 'De-Christianization' became a central aspect of state policy, with the army enforcing the Revolutionaries' ban on Christian practice, and, alongside the enforcement of conscription, decreed on 23 August 1793, this increased popular opposition.

The Vendée on the west coast saw the most sustained opposition. The rebels called themselves the Royal and Catholic Army. Initial royalist success, which benefited from the advantages of fighting in wooded terrain, led to brutal repression, including widespread atrocities by government forces, notably their 'infernal columns', which was an aspect of the way in which the Revolution had become a war on the French people. Underlining the ideological dimension, strong piety was linked to more explicitly anti-Revolutionary violence and support for royalism. This was a conflict of ambushes and massacres, but also of battles. The weakness of government forces in 1792–93, a reflection of their commitment to war with Austria and Prussia, allowed the peasant insurgency to develop and spread, but, in turn, 16,000 troops were sent to the Vendée region later in 1793, and they helped account for the major governmental victories at Cholet (the royalist rebels' military capital) and Le Mans, victories that played the key role in defeating the insurgency, notably by hitting its morale and ending its sense of impetus and purpose. The rebels also faced difficulties in capturing cities, especially Nantes, again a persistent problem for insurgencies: cities tended to be fortified and better defended. The atrocities by the government forces spurred the rebels to activity, but the switch by the government to a more conciliatory stance resulted in some of the rebels agreeing to terms in 1794.

The *Chouans* of Brittany mounted a parallel rising in 1792–1800. They were supported by intense religious piety and loyalty to their exiled priests, and led by the charismatic and physically powerful Georges Cadoudal. He was finally executed in 1804 after a failed attempt to assassinate Napoleon. This struggle was an instance of the way in which the Revolution had spawned a new religious conflict with the adversaries having the same level of faith and commitment on both sides.

Provincial opposition was not only mounted by royalists. The purge of the Girondin *députés* contributed in 1793 to a series of revolts, especially in southern France, revolts termed 'federalist' by the Revolutionaries. Those in Bordeaux, Caen and Marseille were swiftly repressed, but the opposition in Lyon and Toulon was fierce, although overcome. Much of western and southern France was in a state at least close to insurrection from 1792, which was to contribute greatly to the divided political culture of France in the nineteenth century, with these areas most consistently conservative. At the same time, this contrast drew on longer patterns of variations in the extent of governmental power; in particular, much of the south and of the west represented longstanding problems for central government.

Turning against France, the Corsicans, whose island had only been sold by Genoa to France in 1768, requested British protection in 1793. A British fleet arrived the following year, and the French troops on the island were defeated, although Nelson lost an eye in the siege of Calvi. A democratic constitution was established with an elected parliament and a British viceroy, and there was talk of Britain being offered the Crown of Corsica. However, Spain moving to join France and thereby altering the naval situation led the British to withdraw from the Mediterranean and, in 1796, the French reconquered the island.

A more profound change affected France's overseas empire. In February 1794, in response both to the slave rising in Saint-Domingue (Haiti) that had begun in 1791 and to liberal thought in Paris, slavery was abolished in all French colonies. Many of France's colonies were attacked by the British in the war between the two that began in 1793.

A far less serious cause of unpopularity than de-Christianization, but one symptomatic of the disruptive drive for change, was the change in the calendar introduced in 1793. The National Convention had entrusted the task of developing a Republican calendar to a commission headed by Charles-Gilbert Romme (1750–1795), a mathematician. Dating the year retrospectively from the start of the republic in September 1792, with each year commencing at the autumn equinox, the new calendar also changed the weeks and months of the year, with months to be of equal length. Each day was to last ten hours, each made up of a hundred minutes, in turn made up of a hundred seconds.

The general theme of much recent work is the limited appeal of the Revolutionary programme once aristocratic constitutionalism had been replaced by a degree of social and religious radicalism. The Revolutionaries were committed to the new and to modernity, notably in opposition to feudalism and to heredity as a justification for rank, hierarchy and subordination. A sense of the new as both present and inevitable led to a requirement that its promise be implemented. The appropriation, renaming and desecration of sites of royal and religious power, notably palaces, cathedrals and monasteries, were part of this process. Thus, the abbey at Jumièges was demolished, leaving only ruins. On 20 September 1792, royal statues were pulled off pedestals across France, while the royal corpses from Saint-Denis were exhumed and reburied in a common grave in 1793. The urn containing Louis XIV's heart, preserved in the Church of Saint-Paul-Saint-Louis in Paris (now better known as Saint-Paul in the Marais), was melted down and the heart destroyed. The treasures of discarded cathedrals and monasteries were allocated to the Musée national des Monuments Français founded in 1795. Medieval sites frequently reflect much damage from the period, for example the abbey at Cluny.

Secularization entailed a rupture with the role of religion in education, and, in its place, science and mathematics played a greater role, and the new educational institutions, notably the Institut national des Sciences et des Arts, established in 1795, adopted an ideology of nationalism and the spirit of progress. Despite subsequent changes in regime, the Revolution set a pattern of governmental encouragement of a meritocratic society employing useful knowledge. Meanwhile, the idea, nature and process of public history was affected by a pressure for disclosure and free information. There was pressure for open diplomacy and for the publication of information on state finances, and the Revolutionaries made state archives open to the public as sovereignty was derived from the people. The *Archives nationales* were founded in 1790 and, in 1794, a decree made it mandatory to centralize all pre-Revolutionary public and private archives.

The Revolution's challenge to established privilege did not affect only the obviously privileged; regional privileges, corporate and communal rights, and traditional cultural norms were all shattered or, at least, tested, as with the threat to medical independence posed by the unsuccessful attempt to create a system of government-sponsored universal healthcare. The attack on religion was particularly serious, and if European rulers, such as the Emperor Joseph II (r. 1780–1790), the ruler of Austria, had limited the wealth and authority of the Catholic Church, none had assaulted Christian beliefs and practices to the extent of the Revolutionary government. As the superficiality of 'de-Christianization' and the vitality of religious faith in the eighteenth century are increasingly appreciated, so the limited appeal of the Revolutionary message as it developed can be more readily grasped.

OFFICIALLY ADOPTED AS THE FRENCH NATIONAL ANTHEM in 1795, 'La Marseillaise' is known throughout the world as a call to arms and a hymn to freedom. Originally titled 'Chant de guerre pour l'Armée du Rhin' (War Song for the Army of the Rhine), it was written in 1792 as a march following the declaration of war against Austria. It gained its more popular name after being chanted by volunteers from Marseille and inspired a sculpture on the Arc de Triomphe. Banned under both Napoleon and Louis XVIII, it was only permanently reinstated in 1879 but is now one of the most recognizable and stirring anthems, often sung before major national events. Famously it was used as a counterpoint to the German anthem in the film *Casablanca* (1942), and it was sung widely in the aftermath of the 2015 Paris terror attacks.

On 27 July 1794, the prospect, held out by Robespierre in a speech on 26 July, of fresh purges led to the coup of 9 Thermidor, named after the month in the Revolutionary calendar. Denounced in the National Convention as a tyrant, Robespierre and his close allies, including Saint-Just, were arrested at once. Declared outlaws, they were executed the following evening in the Place de la Révolution with no rising mounted to save them. In the 'Thermidorian Reaction', a less radical regime took their place, leading in 1795 to the creation of the Directory government. Ironically, the Thermidorians and Directory can be seen as another form of extremism, that of an extreme ideological centre. The Jacobin Club was closed in 1794–95, while the National Guard, which had been radical from the summer of 1792, became the force of order and helped defeat uprisings in 1795, notably the insurrection of 1 Prairial Year III, a revolt of the poor in Paris on 20 May. Also in 1795, a 'White Terror' in the south took revenge on the Jacobins. Alongside political reaction, there was a cultural turning towards elitism, and against the possibility of a popular culture posed during the Revolution as well as the compulsory virtue and sober uniformity of the Terror. There was also a return to fashions in clothes, while in 1795, the Place de la Révolution was renamed the Place de la Concorde.

The National Convention dissolved itself in November 1795 in order to make way for a new constitution and regime, that of the Directory. Although a bicameral legislature and a system of checks and balances were created, real power rested with the five directors who composed the Directory. Continued foreign war, however, prevented any real stability. The Directory believed foreign war necessary in order to support the army, to please its generals and to control discontent, not least by providing occupation for the volatile generals, whom they found it difficult to manage. Yet, victories led to pressure for further conquests in order to satisfy political and military ambitions and exigencies, and the Directory had to support the war, as well as to deal with the massive deficit inherited from the monarchy, as the issue of *assignats* – paper money – had not solved the problem: the Revolutionary regime could not control its debts, and the *assignats* lost value in the face of serious inflation.

The political 'centre', the base of the Directory, was divided, and, in very difficult circumstances, was under challenge from both Left and Right, and instability was accentuated by both elections and conspiracies. In the coup of 18 Fructidor (4 September 1797), the two moderate directors were removed by their more assertive colleagues, the Chamber was purged of many royalist deputies, and a more Jacobin style of politics was adopted. This 'Second Directory' denied the constitutional royalists gains made in the elections of that March. The different prospects offered by a royalist France had already been thwarted by the failure of attempts to overthrow the Directory in 1795, notably with fighting in Paris on 5 October in which Napoleon Bonaparte (1769–1821) employed his forces to great effect. Far more than the reputed 'whiff of grapeshot' was used to crush the royalists, between 200 and 300 of whom were killed.

The electoral franchise remained very broad and the level of participation was reasonably high. The elections of 1798 produced a large group of radical deputies, only for the Directory to annul many of the results, because the ethos and practice of participatory politics threatened the stability of elite power and helped make the Directory appear unsettled. This both encouraged its overthrow in 1799 and was a major reason why the bourgeois then turned to Napoleon: he safeguarded, if not political freedom, at least the status and power challenged by elections and electioneering. The divisions that were deepened by the Terror, plus the continuation of the war, had made it virtually impossible to establish successfully any sort of stable liberal regime after 1795, and, as a consequence, the outcome of 1799 was always likely, although it might have been a stronger form of civilian rule, rather than that of Napoleon.

Meanwhile, France's military and international positions had improved. The *levée en masse*, a general conscription ordered in 1793, raised large forces, and these were used for offensive operations to a degree that *ancien régime* militia had not been. Ideas of valour, indeed masculinity, were presented in terms of such action. After the chaos of the initial years of the Revolution, there were also major improvements in military organization. Helped in large part by being able to seize resources from the areas in which they were campaigning, armies could operate effectively on several fronts at once, match the opposing forces of much of Europe, take heavy casualties and continue fighting. Although there were major difficulties, notably in logistics, the army was moulded and sustained as a war-winning force, being more successful than Louis XIV had been in his multi-front campaigning in the 1700s. The Allies were defeated in the Austrian Netherlands (Belgium) in 1794, the Netherlands were overrun in 1795, the year in which Prussia and Spain abandoned the war with France, and the conquest of northern Italy by Napoleon in 1796–97 led Austria to abandon the War of the First Coalition in 1797.

However, the Directory faced considerable pressure in the War of the Second Coalition that began in 1798, with Austria, Britain and Russia the key powers involved against France. They proved able to mount a formidable challenge to the Directory, and France faced the strains of a difficult conflict such that the Directory had scant support when it was overthrown by Napoleon in what was ironically a poorly organized coup on 9 November 1799 (18 Brumaire according to the revolutionary calendar). The optimistic hopes of 1789 were long passed. France was still at war and there was no sign that stability would be restored.

9. From Napoleon I to Napoleon III, 1799–1870

In 1800, war dominated national attention, but vaccination against smallpox, introduced into France that year, may have been more significant. Within a decade, half of all babies were being vaccinated. New standards also modified other key aspects of everyday life, producing changes that have lasted until the present. In 1790, the National Assembly adopted a report proposing uniform weights and measures based on an invariable model taken from nature, and, in 1791, adopted as its criterion for the universal measure the *metre*: one ten-millionth of the distance from the North Pole to the Equator. The *kilogramme* and the *litre* were part of this process. Such changes contributed to the idea that France experienced its period of 'Enlightened Despotism' during the 1790s and, more clearly, under Napoleon, who moved from being first consul in 1799 to becoming emperor in 1804, using each time a title with a Roman echo. Ruling until forced by defeat to abdicate in 1814, Napoleon had time to try to implement reform and shape France into modernity. He returned to power in 1815, full of new projects but, again, was forced out by defeat, and this time rapidly so.

Napoleon was born Napoleone Buonaparte, in Corsica, 1769, to a low-ranking noble family that would have been regarded as more Italian than French. For all his egocentric ambition and posturing, Napoleon was genuinely interested in a kind of rational modern administration, and found it appropriate to present himself accordingly. He introduced some worthwhile features of government, notably issuing a new civil law code, the *Code Napoléon* (1804). Napoleon also reorganized financial, local and judicial administration. More generally, the cult and practice of self-conscious modernization was advanced as explaining the logic and value of the Revolutionary and Napoleonic systems. Both cult and practice drew on the rejection of the past seen with the radicals of the Revolution, but also reflected a deliberate engagement with an ideology of efficiency under Napoleon. A greater use of modernization was an aspect of the latter, and, for example, Jean-Antoine Chaptal, minister of the interior from 1800 to 1804, sought to utilize useful information in order to encourage industrial innovation. A chemist, Chaptal was a key figure in the development of industrial policy, publishing his *France industrielle* in 1819. Indeed, much of the modernizing project was realized after Napoleon, as was the case for the crucial development in the mathematical analysis of medical treatments, which did not occur until the 1830s, with Pierre-Charles-Alexandre Louis's statistical assessment of rival therapies.

Napoleon's ideas of rational modernity, however, were often crude, for example his views on economic and financial matters, while he repeatedly undermined his own efforts by his rapacity, militarism and neo-feudalism, the last very much seen with the new imperial nobility. Napoleon was also an opportunist who operated by jettisoning the unpopular aspects of the Revolution, such as the abolition of slavery and the breach with Catholicism. Slavery was restored in 1802, and the entry to France of West Indian black and mixed-race people was prohibited; although, in 1802–3, Napoleon's attempt to crush black independence in Saint-Domingue failed, and Haiti, as a result, became independent in 1804. The decimal calendar was discarded by Napoleon in 1805–6 for commercial and scientific reasons, but also as part of his wider reaction against the Revolution and of his reconciliation with Catholicism, albeit both being very much on his own terms.

These aspects of his rule tend to be forgotten in today's public discussion of Napoleon, especially by those who praise him. They take the surface impression of achievement and fail to notice the underlying reality. Indeed, the ambivalent nature of Enlightened Despotism is captured by Napoleon's policies, not least his preference for war, although we should not be surprised by the fact that Napoleon made both good and bad decisions. He certainly did not really understand compromise, and his system and psyche required force and success, while he relished a warrior cult, as in the celebration of the mythical Celtic poet Ossian in the decoration of his wife the Empress Joséphine's palace at Malmaison. Indeed, Napoleon reconceptualized military honour: in place of dynasticism, his military dictatorship emphasized the honour of dedication and professionalism, both of which were focused on Napoleon and defined by him. The army represented this process, and was the vital means to disseminate the relevant values. Thus, in 1804, 80,000 troops witnessed Napoleon handing out crosses of the newly created *Légion d'honneur* to almost 2,000 troops in an elaborate spectacle staged on the cliffs at Boulogne in which he encouraged soldiers to defend their reputation and the honour of the French name. This is an occasion commemorated by the Column of the Grand Army north of Boulogne, built at the urging and expense of Napoleon's own troops.

Although propaganda presented Napoleon as always in favour of peace, the regime, in practice, celebrated power, not least that of victory, in its activities, iconography and commemoration. The battle of Marengo in 1800, a chaotic victory of improvisation over the Austrians, was crucial to establishing Napoleon's power in Italy, while his defeat of Austrian, Russian and Prussian armies, notably at Ulm (1805), Austerlitz (1805) and Jena (1806), was fundamental to the reorganization of much of Europe. France expanded to include the Low Countries and places further afield. Piedmont and Elba were annexed in 1802, Tuscany and Parma in 1808, Rome, Trieste, Fiume and the Illyrian provinces (Croatia, Slovenia, Istria) in 1809, and Hamburg, Lübeck and Bremen in 1810.

Moreover, Napoleon turned to a new imperial dynasticism. Having crowned himself emperor, he divorced Joséphine in order in 1810 to marry Marie Louise, the daughter of the Emperor Francis I of Austria, formerly the Holy Roman Emperor, Francis II. Thus, the legitimacy of the past was joined to a new legitimacy based on power, and Napoleon's son, 'Napoleon II' (1811–1832), was styled King of Rome. The imperial ambitions of Napoleon are aptly displayed by the tacky lavishness of the palace at Compiègne. In turn, Bourbon palaces he did not favour were demolished, in part for building materials.

The move from a universal message contained within the promise and initial stages of the Revolution was taken further under Napoleon, in part because of the focus on his personal position. Like the Revolutionaries, but with a different conclusion, Napoleon looked back to antiquity, fashioning, in his own iconography and that of the regime, a self-image in terms of the achievements, glamour and status of the ancient world, especially Rome. In doing so, there was a clear counterpointing to the alleged decadence of the Bourbon *ancien régime*. The despoiling of European artworks for the glorification of Paris reflected another instance of the Napoleonic appropriation of the past. In addition, celebratory works were produced, notably by Jacques-Louis David, including *Bonaparte Crossing the Great St Bernard Pass* (1800), *The Consecration of the Emperor Napoleon* (1805–7, see pl. x) and *The Distribution of the Eagle Standards* (1810). Particular victories were celebrated in paintings and the titles awarded to his generals. Meanwhile, France's past continued to be despoiled by the destruction of much of its ecclesiastical heritage. This was particularly the case of the monasteries, as at the Abbey of Saint-Jean-des-Vignes at Soissons, while the Basilica of Saint Martin was destroyed in Tours. Others survived only by being used for non-clerical purposes, such as the Abbey of Fontevraud as a prison, and that of Fontenay as a paper mill.

Napoleon's military legacy in the mid and late 1800s was very mixed. Alongside dramatic victory over Austria and Prussia, naval action and economic warfare failed against Britain, most spectacularly with the naval defeat at Trafalgar in 1805. Napoleon also found Russia a difficult opponent in 1807, notably in the battle of Eylau. This conflict, closing with victory at Friedland and the Treaty of Tilsit of 7 July 1807, was punishing, although it further vindicated the quality of the French military machine. Invaded in 1808, in part in order to establish his brother Joseph on the throne, Spain proved a more intractable opponent, and this was an unnecessary war, as Spain was not earlier opposed to France. Initial French success was followed by a major rebellion, and, although British intervention did not irreversibly succeed until 1813, it helped sustain Spanish opposition to France. Meanwhile, war with Austria in 1809 led to failure for Napoleon at Aspern-Essling, but victory at Wagram. However, the invasion in Russia in 1812, a product of his increased hubris, was a total disaster, with the invading army lost to battle, disease and the winter climate. It was followed by Prussia and then Austria abandoning France, in 1813, and by French troops being heavily defeated at Leipzig in the 'Battle of the Nations' later that year.

For most of Napoleon's reign, the territory of France itself did not experience conflict and occupation. Helped by this, a variety of other developments occurred. Thus, in 1810, the Swiss-born, Paris-based Abraham-Louis Breguet created the first wristwatch

– for Caroline Murat, Queen of Naples – while the *Annales de mathématiques pures et appliquées* became mathematics' first successful specialized journal. Focusing on the teaching of the subject and edited by Joseph Diez Gergonne, a Languedoc teacher, the journal drew heavily on the work of provincial mathematicians, reflecting the broad-based nature of French mathematical culture. Napoleon supported educational reform and was responsible for the idea of the *lycée* (schools for educating the children of the elite); several were soon built in France, including the Lycée Lakanal in Sceaux, the first state-funded boarding school in the rural area around Paris. At the same time, as throughout French history, it is necessary to note the range of experience, and, in the areas of Arras and Saint-Omer in 1802 and 1804, surveys revealed that hardly 35 to 40 per cent of the men were reckoned as knowing how to read and write, and fewer than 5 per cent of the rural population were considered well-educated.

Repeated defeats in 1812–13 created a crisis within France, with falling tax revenues, widespread draft avoidance, a serious shortage of arms and equipment, and a marked decline in the morale and efficiency of officials. The economy was in a parlous state, hit by the effective British blockade and by the loss of European markets, problems that helped ensure that the Allied invasion of France in 1814 saw Napoleon's control over both regime and army rapidly crumble. With Allied forces advancing into the suburbs of Paris, a provisional French government deposed him and, with his marshals unwilling to fight on, he abdicated in April. Following on from a number of such changes in the 1790s, this was the first of a series of nineteenth-century enforced changes of government. The Bourbon claimant, the rather lacklustre Louis XVIII (1755–1824), Louis XVI's elder surviving brother who had long been an exile in Britain, became king: Louis XVII, the son of Louis XVI, had never come to the throne, dying in 1795 while imprisoned.

The generous terms of the Peace of Paris of May 1814 were designed to help Louis XVIII. German hopes of regaining Alsace were not fulfilled, whereas France got her frontiers of January 1792, with some important and favourable border rectifications, including the retention of Avignon, a Papal possession before the Revolution that had been annexed in 1791. In 1814, Napoleon was exiled by the victorious powers to Elba, an island between Corsica and Tuscany, but he was given sovereignty over it, as well as a revenue of two million francs from the French government which, in the event, proved unwilling to pay up. He used the opportunity to improve the situation of the inhabitants, including by roadbuilding and educational reforms, but this was no long-term solution; instead, it was a frustrating lesson in impotence that mocked his greatly inflated sense of his own dignity.

As ever an opportunist, Napoleon escaped the island with a thousand men on 26 February 1815, evading two patrolling French ships and one British one. Having landed near Antibes on 1 March, he rapidly and decisively advanced on Paris, reaching it on 20 March, the regular army refusing to fight him, while the unpopular Louis fled before his arrival. There was opposition in the south and west, but Napoleon was able to reimpose his authority in France fairly easily in what was a swift conquest.

Nevertheless, Napoleon found little enthusiasm for the war that his return launched, and conscription was particularly unwelcome, although he was able to call on veterans whose experience was essentially one of war, and most of whom had seen few opportunities under Louis XVIII. The European powers united to overthrow Napoleon, only for him to pre-empt them by invading Belgium on 15 June, aiming to defeat and drive back the British and Prussian armies there separately. At Quatre-Bras and Ligny, respectively, the French fought them on 16 June, but with no decisive victory, and Napoleon's gamble was crushed at Waterloo on 18 June.

France was then invaded by British, Prussian and Austrian forces, and occupied. The lack of any sustained opposition to the invaders reflected the collapse in Napoleon's popularity. His regime was totally dependent on his main battle army and his prestige; both were now fragile with weakened foundations, and could not prevent collapse. Napoleon tried to rebuild his army and to rally support in Paris, but failed. Waterloo also determined the struggle with counter-Revolutionaries, notably in southern France and the Vendée. The battle led to the revival of royalist militias who supported the Bourbon Louis XVIII, and their activities captured the extent to which civil conflict was part of warfare. In a 'Second White Terror', the targets of the militias were people identified as opponents of the royalists, but the violence also had a religious complexion, notably in Languedoc, with Catholics attacking Protestants, who were portrayed as disloyal. Meanwhile, Napoleon surrendered to a British warship and was subsequently exiled to distant Saint Helena, a British island in the South Atlantic. He would return to France only as a corpse in 1840, when his burial in the Invalides became a way for King Louis Philippe to seek popularity. The next year, for the same reason, a statue of Napoleon was finally placed on the column at Boulogne.

No warrior, Louis XVIII returned to Paris after Waterloo, but the Second Treaty of Paris that November stipulated harsher terms, notably a large indemnity of 700 million francs, the occupation of much of France in order to ensure compliance, and frontier cessions that included what were to be the important Saar and Sambre coalfields, which would have been a useful addition to French resources in the later competition with Germany. Headed by the Duke of Wellington, the 150,000-strong occupation forces, which remained until 1818 when the reparations were repaid, were also a guarantee of Louis's position.

Louis subsequently faced opposition, but so did other regimes in Europe, and what was striking was the resumption of a degree of control and stability, even if monarchy was not particularly popular. The discrediting of Bonapartism by defeat was important to this process, as was the ability to end the occupation, and early; but there were also longer-term issues. In particular, the popularity and impact of the Revolution should not be exaggerated, and, radicalism exhausted and discredited, France swiftly reverted to order and then monarchy, first Napoleonic and then Bourbon, while revolutions elsewhere in Europe in the 1790s were suppressed or forced to depend on French military assistance. Indeed, Napoleon's reordering of the map of Europe was based on his army, and mostly not on popular consent.

Separately, France had achieved many of its military successes as a state that exemplified diverse features that pre-Revolutionary ministers had sought to introduce, and if Napoleon pushed ideas for change further than they had done, many aspects of the *ancien régime* and much of its culture survived under him. Partly as a result, the major changes of the following century were to take place in a society still heavily influenced by privilege and faith, both firmly enmeshed in the fabric of everyday life, while some Napoleonic reforms were reversed, for example divorce legislation in 1816.

Meanwhile, revolutions elsewhere in Europe in the late 1810s, 1820s and early 1830s were suppressed by the coalition of conservative powers consolidated by the Congress of Vienna of 1814–15 and subsequent agreements; and France's influence in Europe waned.

Far from charismatic, Louis XVIII had brought a welcome stability, and while the introduction of limited conscription in 1818 was preceded by heated debates in which concern about the revolutionary potential of the 'nation in arms' was expressed, in practice Louis faced no such crisis. The conscripts were selected by lot, but, as it was possible to arrange a substitute by means of payment, they were mostly from the poor.

Louis's successor in 1824, his brother Charles X (1757–1836), a more controversial figure who offered an attempt at a revived pre-Revolutionary Bourbon monarchy that made no concessions to liberalism, can be approached by tourists through the extensive regalia at Reims from his lavish coronation, which was the basis for an opera by Rossini. Royalist sympathy led to the sculptures of Louis XVI and Marie Antoinette kneeling in prayer in the basilica at Saint-Denis (see pl. IX).

It is easy to present Charles's overthrow in 1830 as inevitable, but the events that year in Paris were no more so in their course and consequence than those that had led the young Charles, then Count of Artois, to flee Paris in 1789. He ironically suffered from the successful capture of Algiers in 1830, which was part of a pattern of resumed expansion that had already taken French forces on a successful intervention in Spain in 1823. The absence of much of the army in 1830 left Charles, in July, vulnerable in the face of three days of disturbances in Paris in response to his refusal to accept election results arising from a clash between the Assembly and the appointment of ministers by the Crown. In response, Charles issued emergency decrees, dissolved the Assembly and cut the size of the electorate, as well as censoring the press. Charles had foolishly turned to Prince Jules de Polignac as leading minister, but he lacked the necessary acumen, while the deficiencies of regulars in the street fighting was an issue, as was a lack of food and ammunition for them. Charles failed to provide leadership, Marshal Marmont did not prove up to the task, and Charles was replaced by the Orléans branch of the royal family in the shape of Louis Philippe, whose father 'Philippe Égalité' had played a role in the overthrow of Louis XVI in 1789–92.

Ruling 'the July Monarchy' until 1848, Louis Philippe (1773–1850) was a more liberal figure than Charles, and his overthrow also was far from inevitable. Instead, the Orléanist years saw considerable economic growth and imperial expansion, including the acquisition of Tahiti, as well as an effective grounding of a new political system that was grounded in the wealthy bourgeoisie. Liberalism was present in the abolition of censorship, as well as the ending, in 1833, of the branding and mutilation of slaves, and giving free black people political and civil rights. New technology included the first French locomotive in 1838. No Charles X, Louis Philippe was willing to incorporate Revolutionary and Napoleonic reforms, but the model was not the Revolution of 1789, still less republicanism, but, rather, the less disruptive English revolution of 1688–89. François Guizot, Louis Philippe's most influential minister from 1840 to 1848 and a Protestant who was very interested in the English model, both historical and contemporary, backed the expansion of public education but was opposed to a further extension of the franchise.

The year 1848, like 1830, was a year of general political upheaval across much of Europe, and France was not immune. This was the 'Spring of the Peoples', with great hopes for the improvement of the lot of the common people, great hopes that had their roots in the Enlightenment, and that mixed anxiety towards modernization alongside the realization that change was inevitable. This year was also the cradle of socialism, as well as a challenge to the power of Austria, the great continental empire that was dictating European diplomacy. As with Vienna in 1848, the extent to which Paris as the capital city was the focus of politicization, and the place where economic grievances were most acute, was important in France. The army had already been used against rebellious silk-weavers in Lyon in 1831 and 1834 and, with great brutality, Paris in 1834; and, in a very different political context, against a

Bourbon rising in the Vendée in 1831 and a Bourbon conspiracy in Brittany in 1832. More recently, France had been hit hard by a savage economic downturn from 1846, with the grain harvest failing in 1846 and 1847, and the resulting rise in the price of bread hurting living standards and industry. In February 1848, rioting began in Paris. Louis Philippe, unwilling to use regular troops to try to destroy the new revolution, fled to England where he died in 1850. Reflecting, as with Napoleon in 1815, the strength of the dynastic drive, Louis Philippe abdicated in favour of his grandson, Philip, Count of Paris, but although there was support for this idea in the National Assembly, public opinion in Paris was opposed and the republicans seized power.

A republic, the Second Republic (after that founded in 1792, retrospectively referred to as the First Republic, which of course ended with the dictatorship of Napoleon), was established. The radicals, who initially dominated the republic, extended the vote to all men, declared a right-to-work and set up national work-shops, a form of publicly funded work, to provide employment. Slavery was abolished in France's colonies. However, elections saw a conservative majority as a result of rural voters who were very different to their more radical urban counterparts, again an aspect of a long-term political rift. Force was then used to sup-press radicalism in Paris with great brutality. In June 1848, when the Parisian workers took to the barricades against the rapid abolition of the national workshops, they were crushed by the minister of war, General Louis-Eugène Cavaignac. There was a clear socio-geographical edge to the counterinsurgency strug-gle as peasant regular troops and 100,000 National Guardsmen (who had refused to defend the king in February) fought their way through the city's barricades against the insurgents' 'Army of Despair'. Over 16,000 troops and 10,000 insurgents were killed and, despite a poorly coordinated response by the government forces, radicalism was crushed. Troops were similarly used in Marseille. This division among the working class was more apparent than Karl Marx's claim that the fighting in Paris was 'the first great battle…between the two classes that split modern society'. There was no foreign intervention on either side.

The situation remained unstable, and it was exploited by Louis Napoleon (1808–1873), the opportunistic nephew of the emperor, who was elected president of the republic. This proved an uneasy cohabitation and, on 2 December 1851, Napoleon overthrew the republic in a *coup d'état*, arresting the political leaders and crushing resistance. Opposition, including in Languedoc, and most notably Provence, was overcome. On 2 December 1852, after a rigged referendum, Louis Napoleon made himself emperor, as Napoleon III, Napoleon II (or the King of Rome) being the son of Napoleon I who died of tuberculosis in 1832 without ever ruling.

As with Napoleon I, Napoleon III came to power in a coup and fell, in 1870, as a result of defeat in war. Meanwhile, there was much in common between the two emperors, with Napoleon III also keen on show and relishing the impression of power. He wished to live lavishly, as the palace at Compiègne, notably the Théâtre Impérial, amply demonstrates; so also with the renovation of the château at Pau. Napoleon's imperial aspirations in building still leave their mark in the boulevards that Baron Haussmann (1809–1891) pushed through Paris, and in the completion of the harbour at Cherbourg, each reflecting an attempt to display and maintain control: the first to make it easier to police Paris, as straight boulevards gave the artillery a clearer field of fire, and the second to provide a base for the new steam-powered fleet that threatened Britain. Maps of Paris showed the new roads and bridges built under Haussmann (see pl. XI), while the city limits were extended in 1859 to incorporate all or parts of twenty-four suburban communes, creating twenty arrondissements. The loss in 1860 of the wall of the farmers-general (built in 1784–91), being a toll boundary rather than a defensive wall, was met with indifference. After the annexation, some urban areas that had fallen out of favour, such as Notre-Dame-des-Champs (near the Luxembourg Gardens), were gentrified and new ones became popular with the middle class, such as the Parc Monceau.

The Napoleonic regime was not grounded in political support and, although not to the same degree as under Napoleon I, elections and their results were manipulated to ensure Napoleon's position. There was, nevertheless, some liberalization from 1859 and, in 1869, a move toward a 'liberal emperor', with ministers answerable to the emperor. It is unclear to what this would have led in time.

Napoleon III was also keen on war and imperial expansion. In order to develop Catholic backing at home, and notably to win support accordingly as an alternative to the Bourbons, Napoleon backed the cause of the Pope in Italy, sending troops to maintain him in the Papal States against radical opposition. Seeking to consolidate his domestic position, and to match the fame of his uncle while drawing on his reputation and example, Napoleon fought Russia in the Crimean War (1854–56) and, far more successfully, Austria in the War of Italian Unification (1859). The contrast presented was with the intervening regimes, and the historical atlas produced by two teachers, Delalleau de Bailliencourt and J. L. Sanis, claimed that the regimes of 1815–48 had not tried to modify the terms of the Congress of Vienna, terms that it alleged humiliated France.

Technology played a major role in Napoleon's military endeavours, notably telegraphs, steamships and trains. As a result, the movement of French troops was greatly speeded up, although Napoleon was apt to try to micro-manage from a distance by telegraph. Thanks to the 1859 campaign, Napoleon in 1860 gained

Nice and Savoy for France, acquisitions it has retained since, except during the Second World War. He also sent troops to Mexico in 1861–67, and considered intervention in the American Civil War against the Union side in 1862, although Britain's refusal to join in led him to prefer prudence.

The western strategy came to an end with the withdrawal of troops from Mexico, as Napoleon sought, instead, to respond to Prussia's growing power for, in 1866, Prussia defeated Austria and gained dominance over Germany. Fearful of Prussia's strength, Napoleon was determined to prevent it from taking over the southern German states – Baden, Bavaria, the Palatinate and Württemberg – by leading them into the German Confederation, as they had been brought into a new customs union in 1869. Otto von Bismarck, the German chancellor, felt that war with France might be necessary in order to secure such a union. However, in a total contrast with his prestigious position in 1859, Napoleon allowed himself to be outmanoeuvred by Bismarck in 1870. Public opinion in France and Germany, which had played a role in creating an atmosphere favourable for war, was manipulated when Bismarck edited a telegram recording a meeting between Wilhelm I of Prussia and the French ambassador, Count Benedetti, at Bad Ems, in order to make their discussion over a Hohenzollern candidature for the vacant Spanish throne appear acrimonious and threatening. Certain leading figures in Paris, notably the foreign minister, Agénor, Duke of Gramont, a minister of the old nobility, were easily provoked, or simply lost all sense of proportion. Hostile to growing Prussian power, Napoleon brought matters to a head by declaring war on 16 July 1870, and did so without allies.

In the event, the Franco-Prussian War rapidly brought down Napoleon. The Prussians benefited from the respective size of the armed forces, which was a consequence of the growth rate in France's population being lower than those of Britain and

Germany, which was of fundamental consequence for French history and reflected both fertility within France and the results of the heavy loss of life in the wars of 1792–1815. In 1870, the French also had no equivalent to the reserves of the Prussian *Landwehr*, in part because political opposition in the *Corps législatif* had hamstrung the attempt in the 1868 Military Law to create a 400,000-strong reserve of the *Garde nationale mobile*. For political and military reasons, there was to be no well-trained second army like the *Landwehr*: distrustful of his adventurism, republican opponents of Napoleon were dubious about the value of a larger army, and military spending was actually cut in January 1870. The regular army was not keen on expansion because it feared that a large number of conscripts would dilute military quality, but a smaller population (and lower growth rate) than that of Germany reduced the pool for the army and underlined the damage done to France by Prussia's success in unifying Germany in 1866.

In light of the relative potential numbers, it would have been sensible for the French to take the initiative, before the Prussians could call up the reserves and link their forces with those from southern Germany, but there was no adequate plan for war with Prussia. The improvisation that had worked against the slower-moving (and more distant) Russians in 1854 and Austrians in 1859 was no longer appropriate, and experience in Algeria, Mexico and the Papal States in the 1860s was no preparation for a conflict in which a powerful Prussia was to seize and retain the initiative. None of these conflicts provided familiarity with mass mobilization and warfare, or in manoeuvring against large numbers of well-trained, led, equipped and gunned forces. Moreover, colonial expeditions were not the best preparation for coordinating corps on a European battlefield.

In 1870, Napoleon proved a particularly maladroit leader, wilfully confident in his own judgment, but the calibre of his generals was also poor, and they proved unable to match the German tempo, in part because they mishandled the attempt to gain the strategic advantage by taking the first step. Instead, the French failed to sustain the initiative and fell back. Most of the war was to be fought on French soil, which was a damaging blow to French morale, while the outnumbered French, who adopted a generally defensive posture, were repeatedly outmanoeuvred by more adept German commanders.

The two main French armies were defeated separately. Marshal Achille Bazaine, the commander of the Army of the Rhine, retreated into the extensive fortifications at Metz, thus surrendering both mobility and an opportunity, first, to block the Prussians and, later, to prevent envelopment. Bazaine's subsequent operations were lacklustre and allowed the Prussians the opportunity to destroy the Army of Châlons being assembled under Marshal Patrice de MacMahon. Its advance towards Metz was a risky manoeuvre, because Napoleon assured MacMahon that Bazaine was pushing towards him from Metz. When it became clear that this was not true, and that the Prussian field marshal Helmuth von Moltke was preparing to encircle him, MacMahon tried to retreat to safety, but was trapped at Sedan by the rapidly advancing Prussians who also gained control of the surrounding hills. Under heavy artillery fire, the French surrendered on 2 September. In thirty-six hours at Sedan, the Prussians fired 35,000 shells. Aside from Napoleon, 83,000 troops were taken prisoner; 21,000 had already been captured in the battle. Bismarck hoped that Napoleon's surrender would lead to the end of French resistance, but a new republican government, the basis of the Third Republic which lasted until 1940, was formed in order to fight on.

Under Napoleon III there had been significant economic growth, notably with the spread of the railways. France is a larger country than Britain and had less available coal, but, with the development of the metallurgical industry and the use of coal and iron resources, the railway system was created. The first railway opened between Andrézieux and Saint-Étienne in 1827, in order to move coal to river barges, and a passenger service followed in 1835. As a result of government caution, there were far fewer miles of track completed than in Britain by 1842 – 300 to 1,900 – but a plan of that year agreed that the government would contribute heavily to the cost of railways and, by 1848, 2,000 miles of track were in operation. The great breakthrough occurred in the 1850s and 1860s, not only with more mileage, but also a network, although not yet a truly integrated one due to the multiplicity of companies and to a system of converging on Paris. In 1871, over 23,000 kilometres (14,000 miles) were in operation and, by 1914, 60,000 kilometres (37,000 miles). Railways changed the local, regional and national geographies of France, not least as towns that had been important for river trade and/or as bridging points or road junctions were bypassed. Nevertheless, alongside railways, canals were still important, including that, begun in 1783, from the Rhine to the Saône. When completed in 1833, this linked northern and southern France by joining the Rhine to the Rhône.

As in Britain, the 1850s proved more dynamic than the 1840s: the production of coal and iron increased, as did the installation of steam engines, although growth in the 1860s was even more significant. France was changing as an economy, with implications for its society and politics, and urbanization developed, notably in Paris. The idea of progress was presented by the philosopher, radical and rationalist reformer Auguste Comte (1798–1857) in his *Système de politique positive* (1851–54), which advanced the theory of a multi-stage approach in which sciences moved from a theological to a metaphysical stage, and then on to a positive or experimental one in which rational enquiry would open the way to understanding.

Drioux and Leroy's *Atlas d'histoire et de géographie* (1867) sought to meet educational requirements in accordance with governmental directives and the maps emphasized French territorial extent, not least under Charlemagne and Napoleon I, while one of the '*départements réunis*' under Napoleon III, a reference to his gains from Sardinia/Piedmont, made it clear that he was a worthy ruler. However, alongside Napoleon III's encouragement of development, including stimulating industry and trade, his total failure in foreign policy and war in 1870 brought the Napoleonic episodes to a close.

The imperial project has left memorials across France. Linking the two emperors is Pontivy, which was chosen by Napoleon I as the strategic commercial and military centre of Brittany, and which in 1804 adopted the name Napoleonville. Napoleon III not only visited the town with Empress Eugénie in 1858, he gave a substantial sum from his personal purse for the building of the new Église Saint Joseph at the heart of a grid of streets laid out according to his predecessor's original plans. The layout of the new town of Pontivy, with its grid of streets named after Napoleonic victories and its huge square, originally a cavalry parade ground, is redolent of the imperial project, as conceived by the first and completed by the third Napoleon.

After Napoleon III, there would be no further kings or emperors of France. Having toyed twice with the concept of a republic, from this point forward the people could no longer rely on a regal figurehead to bolster a sense of national identity and unity.

10. The Third Republic, 1870–1939

The Third Republic may have run from defeat in 1870 to defeat in 1940 but, in between, there was, for France, unprecedented economic and imperial growth, as well as considerable sophistication as a liberal and democratic society. Many of the older buildings in French towns date from this period, and it also provides much of what are now seen as the most attractive and interesting features of French culture, notably in painting. The start was far less auspicious, as the republic was proclaimed in Paris on 4 September 1870 as a Government of National Defence by a group of republican politicians responding to the crisis of the continuing war with Prussia. With Paris soon after besieged, the provisional government moved to Tours.

The Franco-Prussian War meanwhile had not developed as anticipated by the Germans. As they advanced into the French interior after victory at Sedan, they were confronted by a more disparate opposition, with newly raised forces. Although these *francs-tireurs* (irregulars) were often relatively easy to defeat in battle, their resistance prevented the Germans from gaining the end to the war they required, not least due to the logistical strain of the continuing war. They responded to *francs-tireurs* with harsh action, including shooting prisoners and burning down settlements. Relying on terror, their army lacked a political remedy to the resistance. Fortunately for Germany, the republican government, in a freezing cold winter and with besieged Paris under damaging German bombardment, accepted terms in March 1871. Indeed, the Germans had agreed an armistice on 28 January, so as to ensure elections that would establish a legitimate French government able to negotiate.

The peace included the German annexation of Alsace bar Belfort, which had held out, and of part of Lorraine, which for the French constituted a significant loss of territory, industrial raw materials and industrial capability. Until an indemnity was paid in 1873, German troops remained in France. Meanwhile, in Alsace-Lorraine, the Germans imposed a new order. It leaves few signs today, other than the large neo-Gothic-style public buildings, railway stations and barracks seen in centres of government, notably Strasbourg and Metz. The latter became a major garrison centre, its rail links developed in order to help German mobilization. Much of the population left for what remained France, including about 50,000 people from Metz, while the family of Alfred Dreyfus, the central figure in the Dreyfus Affair, left Mulhouse in Alsace for Paris. Maps of France drove home the lesson of failure, especially Lamothe's *Carte des agrandissements successifs de la France sous la monarchie, la république et l'empire* (1873), which showed the territory gained at successive periods and then lost under Napoleon III. In case the message was not sufficiently clear, the map's text added:

En résumé, la France a reçu: 85 départements et demi plus l'Algérie des Bourbons, la moitié d'un département de la 1ère République, 3 départements de Napoléon III. D'autre part, par le fait de Napoléon III, puis de la République, la France a perdu 3 départements et demi, les plus riches de son territoire. [In summary, France received: 85 and a half departments plus Algeria from the Bourbons, the half of a department from the 1st Republic, 3 departments from Napoleon III. On the other hand, by the defeat of Napoleon III, then of the Republic, France lost 3 and a half departments, the richest in its territory.]

The elections to the National Assembly, held on 8 February 1871, had produced a monarchist majority. Meeting in Bordeaux, it elected Adolphe Thiers (1797–1877) 'Chief of the Executive Power of the French Republic', with oversight of the process of drawing up a new constitution. Very differently, the Paris Commune, a mostly working-class radical movement, took power in Paris and issued radical decrees ranging from the separation of Church and state to the abolition of nightwork in bakeries. The lack of a middle ground between the two sides ensured that the army of the new republican government was ordered to attack, fighting beginning on 18 March over the control of cannon. After extensive street conflict (see pl. XIV), in which about 10,000 Parisians were killed and sites of conventional authority, such as the Tuileries Palace and the Palais Royal, were set on fire, the Commune was suppressed in May. About the same number were promptly shot, including at the Mur des Fédérés (Communards' Wall) in the cemetery of Père Lachaise: earlier, the Communards had shot their hostages. Other Communards were imprisoned, including at Fort Liédot on the Île d'Aix. With the government based for a while in Versailles, the people of Paris were left feeling intimidated and with a difficult and divisive collective memory. The physical intimidation of the city included the building of Sacré-Coeur on the hill of Montmartre, a church intended to proclaim the presence of religion (see pl. XV).

Stability for the Third Republic was slowly gained, albeit in the face of considerable difficulties. The Société d'Instruction Républicaine helped instil the liberal, republican values of the Third Republic in the 1870s, but, like the government, encountered serious problems. Difficulties included monarchist claimants: Bourbon, Orléanist and, less strongly, Napoleonic, and the first,

Charles X's grandson, the prospective 'Henry V', could have become king in 1871 had he been more accommodating. Anti-republican politicians dominated the early years. There was also uncertainty over the position of the military, notably the possibility in 1888–89 of a coup by General Georges Boulanger, a charismatic strongman who, in the event, did not rise to the challenge. In the end, although monarchy long remained a prospect, the republicans prevailed in the late 1870s, and with a political system that was not under aristocratic control.

The 1875 constitution had created a more broadly based political system, with a universal male franchise, a parliamentary regime, and a president who was essentially ceremonial and lacked the capacity to create a system comparable to that produced by Napoleon III. Politically there appeared to be chaos and the Third Republic was a succession of largely short-term ministries, but there was fundamental stability provided by controlling power brokers in Paris and in the provinces.

Meanwhile, France was greatly changing. Maps of rural France recorded the spread of rail across the country and the resulting potential for a national economy. The maps did not record the enormous strains caused by international economic competition, notably agricultural imports from the New World, and economic problems caused large-scale emigration, notably from Brittany. In addition, an epidemic of phylloxera (pale yellow aphid-like insects) hit vineyards very hard from 1863, with wine production falling from 84.5 million hectolitres (1.9 billion gallons) in 1875 to 23.4 million (515 million gallons) in 1889. In 1880–1914, the share of global manufacturing output for France fell below Russia and drastically below Germany, but the period saw large-scale, coal-based industrialization, and notably in the north-east cities of Douai, Roubaix, Lens, Lille and Valenciennes. Working-class politics became closely linked to this industrialization. Coal also fed the expansion of the textile industry, and the population rose greatly in the Nord, which was depicted with a harsh realism in Émile Zola's novel *Germinal* (1885), part of his epic series of social realism. Set in the pits, it described the difficulties of pushing carts underground and the miners' life of poverty. In the novel, which Zola based on visits to the mining towns in 1884, visits that included going down a pit, a miners' strike is brutally suppressed.

A KEY ELEMENT OF FRENCH CULTURAL MEMORY is the idea that many of the nation's ancient techniques and products can be traced back to the very specific condition in which they were first created. The idea of *terroir* is part of this, although recent research suggests that it is a relatively recent term. It has been adopted by many French cultural institutions to describe a unique link to the land and place of production, which can be detected in the intrinsic essence of the produce. A wine from Bordeaux or the Loire Valley or a type of cheese from Roquefort or Morbier, for example, can be protected internationally by the *appellation d'origine contrôlée*. The influence of *terroir* means that wines such as Champagne from the area surrounding Reims are utterly unique and that a similar wine from elsewhere cannot use the term. France remains one of the largest producers of wine in the world.

Coal was increasingly moved by rail, rather than canal, but a very different use of rail was offered by the movement of the wealthy to new recreational destinations, such as the seaside resorts of Deauville and Le Touquet. With train services from Paris from the 1860s, Nice became the major holiday destination of those taking the train south across France. More generally, directly through travel, which was much enhanced by the rail system, and indirectly, through publications and paintings, there was a discovery of the diversity of France, particularly in the case of the coast through painters visiting Normandy and Brittany. On the Riviera, the light, vivid colours, exciting allure and difference from skies and scenes further north attracted painters such as Renoir, Monet, Signac and Matisse. To the west, in 1876, Cézanne stayed in L'Estaque, a fishing village near Marseille, capturing the impact of the strong Mediterranean light in scenes painted outdoors. There was also an engagement with rural France and the flatlands. The Barbizon School, located near Fontainebleau, was influenced by the paintings of the English artist John Constable as well as by the spectacular scenery. The French landscape offered a neo-Romantic appeal to all those seeking solace in nature. From 1886, Gauguin developed, at Port Aven in Brittany, a radical new approach to art through a synthesis of colour and form, which allowed him to invest with a monumental dignity the harsh lives of the Breton peasants, and to adopt and celebrate the popular religious art of the region. The School of Pont Aven included Paul Sérusier and Émile Jourdain, whose more picturesque images of traditional costumes and customs launched a tourist industry of curious Parisian train travellers. Very differently, in 1895 the Besançon-born Lumière brothers patented their own cinematograph, allowing large numbers of people to simultaneously view their projected motion pictures that year. They also made advances in colour photography.

OF ALL OF THE TECHNICAL AND CULTURAL DEVELOPMENTS that have emerged from France, the one perfected by the Lumière brothers in Lyon is one of the greatest. While the date of the first filming is shrouded in debate, on 22 March 1895 the Lumières presented their invention with a screening in Paris at the Society for the Development of the National Industry. There, an audience of two hundred people watched the appropriately titled *Arrival of a Train at La Ciotat Station*. Ever since, France has been at the vanguard of developments in the medium of film. From the early works of Georges Méliès and Abel Gance's six-hour *Napoléon* (1927) to the New Wave cinema of the 1960s and a vibrant domestic realism of the 1980s and 1990s, French cinema has often been seen as a counterpoint to the more mainstream Hollywood. The Cannes Film Festival, held every year in the south, gives the Palme d'Or to the best film of the year.

Stability was endangered when the Dreyfus Affair exploded, making it difficult for a decade from 1894 to contain political rivalries. Underlying anti-Semitic feelings helped ensure that religious differences were also to the fore. The army's mistaken conviction of Alfred Dreyfus, a Jewish officer (who had earlier suffered anti-Semitism in his career), for spying for the Germans, and its subsequent cover-up of evidence pointing towards an officer of supposedly more estimable stock, caused a national scandal (see pl. XVII). The army itself, very differently to the 1790s, was a conservative force. There was a tradition of promotion from the ranks of enlisted men to those of junior officers, but it became much less significant in the 1890s and 1900s, and the officer corps became more socially exclusive. The army also acted against organized labour, firing on demonstrating textile workers at Fourmies in the Nord in 1891. The use of the army against civilians had fallen after 1871, but it rose from 1890 due to the fear of organized labour. Units usually followed their orders, although in 1907 there was a mutiny in Narbonne when troops from the region refused to act against a winegrowers' demonstration that reflected the problems caused by phylloxera.

The Dreyfus Affair was different: it became a crisis over the character, role and loyalty to the republic of the entire army and over the nature of the nation. The Dreyfusards claimed that the army was run by officers sympathetic to clerical interests, and not to the republic; the anti-Dreyfusards saw the army as the symbol of French nobility and honour, which it sought to protect. Wild talk of purging or defending the army weakened and confused the response to Britain in the Fashoda Crisis of 1898 over the control of Sudan. In 1899, Dreyfus was retried and found guilty anew despite the evidence of his innocence. Dreyfus was then pardoned in an attempt to still the crisis, being finally exonerated in 1906 and serving in the First World War. The Dreyfus Affair had posed the threat of court martial for the senior military, but also of a coup. In turn, in the early 1900s, the government, suspicious of the clerical sympathies of the army, used the police to spy on officers and manipulated promotion accordingly, allegedly encouraging Freemasons, which led to a press furore in 1904. In 1905, the government imposed the legal separation of Church and state and religious freedom. The government funding of religious groups ended while religious buildings were made state property.

THE NAME OF CÉSAR RITZ (1850–1918) is forever linked with ideas of wealth and exquisite taste. Originally from Switzerland, he worked at the Savoy in London before, in 1898, opening his eponymous hotel in a seventeenth-century building overlooking the Place Vendôme in Paris. His head chef was Auguste Escoffier, who codified much of what is now seen as typical French *haute cuisine*. Ever since its opening, the Ritz has been synonymous with opulence and luxury, hosting visiting dignitaries, presidents and stars. Coco Chanel (1883–1971) lived at the hotel for thirty-four years and today there is a suite named in her honour.

By then, the establishment of the Third Republic in 1870 appeared to be the last in a series of regime and constitutional changes going back to 1789 that had led to new public ideologies, and to new histories accordingly. As with most public history of a controversial type, these new histories focused on the recent past, for example the Commune. It was particularly necessary to justify the most recent changes, a process that was to be repeated after constitutional transformations in 1940, 1944 and 1958. Republicans and their rivals sought to rework their recent history in order to provide acceptable accounts for the present, for example of the 1789 Revolution shorn of Jacobin extremism. This can be seen in the Monument aux Girondins erected in Bordeaux, a monument that honoured local politicians executed by the Jacobins. The Third Republic rested on a rejection of earlier monarchical systems, notably Napoleon III's Second Empire. At the same time, this discussion of earlier French history was broader than simply a focus on rejection of the previous regime or regimes. The republican tradition in France emphasized the overcoming of domestic and foreign threats, and this led to a stress on the indivisibility of the state and the universality of its powers within its boundaries. Thus, a historically grounded nationalism was not a monopoly of the Right.

French history was actively contested, not least in the naming and renaming of streets and squares. Catholic legitimists strongly challenged the centenary of the Revolution in 1889 as part of their incessant assault on the Third Republic. The Catholic account looked back to the Middle Ages, but engaged fully in the politics of the moment as Catholicism had become more strident as a result of the eventual rejection of liberalism by Pope Pius IX (r. 1846–1878). This was another aspect of a key theme in French history: the extent to which developments in France were dependent on those outside. The doctrine of the Immaculate Conception of the Virgin Mary (1854) was followed by the bull *Syllabus Errorum* (1864), which criticized liberalism, and by the convocation of the

First Vatican Council (1869–70), which issued the declaration of Papal Infallibility.

Catholicism was not in retreat in France and, instead, there was a demonstration of the Catholic presence with church-building, most dramatically with Sacré-Coeur in Paris, but also with the new Basilica of Saint Martin in Tours and that of Notre-Dame-de-Fourvière on a hilltop in Lyon. Sacré-Coeur was in part financed by means of pilgrimages to the Basilique du Sacré-Coeur in Paray-le-Monial, which began in 1873, a year that also saw the first major pilgrimage to Lourdes, the site, from 1858, of visions of the Virgin Mary seen by Bernadette Soubirous. These pilgrimages were organized by the *Assomptionistes*, an anti-secular Catholic movement. At Lourdes, an underground crypt, built in 1866, was the prelude to a large basilica built in 1871–83. Moreover, medieval sites such as the abbey at Vézelay were revived.

Prejudice and history were mobilized and notably so with *Union nationale*, the Catholic political movement founded in 1892 by Théodore Garnier, which (falsely) claimed that Jews, Freemasons and Protestants were running the Third Republic and needed to be overthrown. The emancipation of the Jews by the Revolutionaries in 1791 was presented as a deliberately anti-Catholic step, and one that condemned both Jews and Revolutionaries. Priests, such as Léon Dehon, played a role in an anti-Semitism that looked toward the Dreyfus Affair. An apparently exemplary nationalist-historical pedigree was found in the late nineteenth century by Catholic conservatives in Joan of Arc's struggle, a struggle given a pronounced religious dimension, and with Joan treated as a providential figure. The gilded bronze equestrian statue of Joan by Emmanuel Frémiet in the Place des Pyramides in Paris, inaugurated in 1874, was a key point for mass demonstrations by Right-wing nationalists, as it is again today, and Joan's struggle was a theme later much used by the Nazi-collaborating Vichy government in the Second World War.

Supporters of the Third Republic favoured tracing the origins of France to the Gauls. In contrast, Conservative opponents, emphasizing a Catholic identity for the nation and Papal links, focused on the Germanic invaders who overthrew imperial Rome, and did so notably because of the baptism of Clovis as France's first Catholic monarch. With religion pushed to the fore as a key factor in national identity, Catholic activism also contributed to the secular response.

In turn, the later use of this period repeatedly served political strategies. In 2006, President Jacques Chirac praised the vindication of Dreyfus a century earlier. In doing so, Chirac, a figure of the Right, signalled his opposition to more toxic and long-lasting aspects of the Right-wing legacy. Drawing a line between the established Right and the *Front national*, Chirac showed that the former was the appropriate custodian of the republican legacy, a point long contested by the Left. This was linked to Chirac disassociating the republic from Vichy. Attacking anti-Semitism served both purposes.

The deployment of memory in the late nineteenth century in part focused on the recent defeat at the hands of Germany. Pierre Denfert-Rochereau, 'The Lion of Belfort', who had mounted a successful defence against German siege in 1870–71, gave his name to many public sites, while a lion was carved into a rockface at Belfort as a monument. Auguste Rodin's sculpture *The Call to Arms* (1879, see pl. XVI) commemorated the defence of Paris, and the *Ligue des patriotes*, founded in 1882, staged regular pilgrimages to battle sites. In the 1900s, books by the novelist Maurice Barrès emphasized the place of Alsace-Lorraine in the French soul, and he became president of the *Ligue* in 1914. Somewhat differently in style, the *Atlas Melin Historique et Géographique* (1895), which was designed for students, focused on the struggle between France and the German lands. More generally, past divisions within

French policy, for example the views of the *dévots* in the 1620s and their opposition to Richelieu, were ignored.

THE TOUR DE FRANCE (see pl. XXI) is one of the world's great annual sporting events with a TV audience of many millions. The most prestigious cycling race in the sporting calendar each year, it follows a similar yet always different route around France (although sometimes starting in another country) for a month in the summer. Le Tour holds a special place in the hearts of the French nation, among whom cycling remains a hugely popular sport and pastime, and is an important projection of France abroad. The race was conceived by the editor and businessman Henri Desgrange as a means of filling the pages of his magazine *L'Auto* and the famous *maillot jaune* (yellow jersey) worn by the race leader is yellow to match the colour of the magazine's pages. The first race took place in 1903 and followed the coast and borders of France as much as possible, starting in Paris and navigating the country in a clockwise fashion. Today, it ends in a sprint finish up the cobbles of the Champs-Élysées. At the time of writing, there hasn't been a French winner of the race since 1985.

Meanwhile, France had won a new empire, mostly in Africa, but also in South-east Asia and the Pacific. Modern African states brought under French control included Algeria, Morocco, Tunisia, Mauretania, Senegal, Guinea, Dahomey, Chad, Burkina Faso, Niger, Mali, the Central African Republic, Congo-Brazzaville and Djibouti. In South-east Asia, the equivalents were Vietnam, Cambodia and Laos. France also had colonies in the Caribbean and the Indian Ocean. Imperial expansion was presented as natural, necessary and beneficial. Thus, in their *Atlas historique* (1900), H. Vast and G. Malleterre, both of whom taught at the military academy, wrote:

L'Algérie, avec la Tunisie, est le prolongement de la France. Il s'y forme un peuple nouveau, de race latine. Elle procure des débouchés sérieux à notre industrie, à notre commerce, à notre marine marchande….C'est une terre d'entraînement pour notre armée et de colonisation pour notre population. [Algeria with Tunisia is an extension of France. A new people of the Latin race is forming there. Algeria will be an important aid to our trade and merchant marine….It is a land of recruitment for our army and of colonization for our people.]

The continued occupation of Algeria, the key colony in North Africa which had been invaded back in 1830, involved the most effort. The French employed ethnography to convince themselves that Algerian culture was not just Muslim but also primitive in thought, organization and practice. This justified imperialism, offering an alternative element more appropriate to the Third Republic than the theme of Christian striving.

The long-term prospects for the Third Republic appeared good in 1914. Alongside economic growth, there had been a settlement of differences with Britain in 1904 with the *Entente cordiale*, but external factors yet again proved crucial. France did not want war, but its military agreement with Russia, although there was no joint war plan between them, led Germany to fear war on two fronts. Germany planned to use speed in the manner that had enabled Prussia to defeat Denmark, Austria and France in 1864–71. Russia's defence-in-depth led German planners to focus on defeating France before turning against Russia (the same course would followed in 1940–41). Encouraged by the example of 1870–71, the Germans assumed that their better-prepared forces would win regardless of French actions.

After Germany declared war on Russia on 1 August 1914, France became the key element for the Germans, who issued an unacceptable ultimatum that France declare neutrality and provide guarantees for this neutrality, steps that would have destroyed the alliance with Russia and made France appear a worthless ally for any other power. The guarantees included its forts at Toul, Verdun and elsewhere, which would have left France highly vulnerable. France's refusal led the Germans to declare war on 3 August.

In the opening campaign of the First World War, a German invasion, successfully mounted through Belgium, nearly succeeded, but the Germans neglected to predict that the French would attack out of their defensive positions. The Sixth Army launched from Paris, initiating the Battle of the Marne. Here, the overextended, exhausted, badly commanded and poorly deployed Germans were stopped and forced to pull back from their position near Paris. Operating on internal lines, and using rail, trucks, buses and taxis, the French could redeploy in a way that the Germans, operating on exterior lines and without transport, could not. In turn, a large-scale French offensive into Lorraine had failed with heavy casualties, notably with infantry blown apart by German artillery.

Thereafter, France fought the war with part of its territory occupied, which encouraged the French to believe that it was necessary to launch offensives. These were unsuccessful, but France held steady, not least in the face of German assaults. Thus, in 1916, seeking to break French will, the Germans attacked at Verdun, a fortress that had great symbolic significance for the French. They planned to advance rapidly on a front of their own choice to capture territory, which the French would then suffer heavy losses trying to retake, but German effectiveness was less than they had assumed. While the French took heavy casualties, 378,000 dead, their willpower was not broken and they also inflicted heavy losses. Moreover, they were able to maintain the movement of supplies into Verdun via what became known as the *voie sacrée* (sacred way) from Bar-le-Duc. Also in 1916, but attacking on the Somme, Corporal Louis Barthas wrote of an Anglo-French bombardment:

> No matter how accustomed we were to the cannonade's rumble, a storm like this rattled our brains, burrowed into our skulls, pressed down upon our chests with a pervasive anguish...more cannon shots were fired in one night than in a whole campaign of Napoleon's.

In 1917, as in 1915, France took the offensive while the Germans rested on the defensive on the Western Front. The heavy costs of the totally unsuccessful Champagne offensive of 1917, named, after its commander, the Nivelle offensive, led to much disaffection in the French army, and, indeed, to a degree of mutiny. However, these did not develop into a major crisis, as happened in Russia in the run up to the October Revolution. Instead, General Philippe Pétain (1856–1951), the 'Lion of Verdun', was appointed commander-in-chief and restored morale, and an improvement in conditions within the army quietened the situation. In 1918, although under great pressure, the French held off the renewed German attacks.

Confronting the strain of war, the government took control of bread prices, while state-supervised consortia directed the allocation of supplies in crucial industries. For example, government-directed shoe and chemical industries were created. Unlike in Germany, there was an appropriate level of care for civilian needs and, thus, morale. France's membership of the alliance against Germany was significant: the loss of production to German occupation was compensated for by the supply of coal, iron and steel by Britain, while economic links with America were also important.

Yet, during the war, there was a slow-moving political crisis, even though the idea of national unity in the defence of an endangered people still held traction. As part of the crisis of legitimation that the costly intractability of the war was causing, there was a series of strikes in early 1917, and growing opposition in the Socialist Party to participation in the government, which had been based since 1914 on the idea of a *union sacrée* (sacred union) of all the parties. The strains of the war were important in the fall of three ministries in 1917, and there was interest among some politicians in peace with Germany, but this was treated as treasonable. In 1917, Georges Clemenceau (1841–1929), a radical politician who was president of the Senate committee for war and foreign affairs, attacked other politicians he saw as unpatriotic. That November, he became prime minister and war minister. Clemenceau declared, 'No more pacifist campaigns....Nothing but the war', and pressed for '*la guerre intégrale*', a focus on the mobilization of national resources to ensure that war was total. Later seen as the 'father of victory', Clemenceau added a powerful strain of authoritarianism to the war economy, focusing industry on the war effort. Those suspected of defeatism, including Joseph Caillaux, a former prime minister, were arrested.

In 1918, the Socialists launched a strong attack on Clemenceau, and the *union sacrée* was formally abandoned. However, despite British concern about the possibility of France collapsing, French political and public support for the war was strong, and indeed grew as the chance of defeat re-emerged in the face of new German attacks. A large-scale strike in Paris came to an end as trade union officials, fearing national defeat and revolution, moved back from the brink. The Allies defeated Germany later that year, with French forces playing a significant part in the final offensive.

The overall burden of the war was very heavy. Indeed, with the heavy losses drawn from across all of France, 27 per cent of men between the ages of eighteen and twenty-seven died in the war, and 1.4 million in total. Large numbers of women and children replaced conscripted rural farmworkers, and 600,000 women were left widowed. Battle sites, war memorials, cemeteries and museums record the human cost and can be seen in every French town, but the war can be grasped mostly clearly in the battlefield near Verdun, notably at the Ossuaire de Douaumont and the Musée-Mémorial de Fleury, the forts of Douaumont, Souville and Vaux, and the shattered landscape. The Verdun battle leaves its mark on war memorials elsewhere, and in rues or boulevards de Verdun in many towns and villages. Streets and squares were also named after Marshal Foch and other wartime figures. The Historial de la Grande Guerre at Péronne is a particularly impressive museum. The devastation of the war to the communities of north-eastern France, notably through bombardment, can be seen in the townscapes of cities such as Reims, with the devastation most obvious in the form of the counterpart: post-war rebuilding.

France played a major role in the subsequent peace settlement, hosting the conference at Versailles, in a response to the humiliating peace of 1871. In the distribution of territories, France gained Alsace-Lorraine and African territories (Togo and Cameroon) from Germany, and Syria and Lebanon as League of Nations mandates from the Turks. France also played a leading part in the containment of the Soviet Union: involvement in the Russian Civil War in 1919–21 failed, but the Poles were helped to block Soviet expansion in 1920.

Meanwhile, concern about communism became prominent in French politics. Elections in November 1919 led to victory for the *Bloc national*, a Right-wing coalition, which thwarted the campaign for women's suffrage, and, instead, in an effort to strengthen the government, took measures to encourage a higher birth rate. The provision of contraceptive information was made illegal in 1920. Meanwhile, in opposition, and against the background of large-scale strikes, notably in the railways in May 1920, the Socialist Party divided that year, part becoming a Communist Party.

The 1920s saw both an unprecedented wave of strikes and recovery after the devastation of the world war, with fiscal stability by the late 1920s, including the return of the franc to the gold standard. Recovery was matched by novelty. Thus, the spreading use of the motor car affected the landscape and experience of France, both rural and urban, and provided new images of fashionability and modernity (see pl. XX). The dominance of the railway was thereby challenged. With this, and the related contest between coal and oil, came a tension that was significant for trade unions and the nature of the political economy. A further dimension to novelty was added by the growing fashionability of aircraft. A more streamlined ethos and style was important to design, but did not have a comparable impact on culture.

However, the 1930s brought the Depression, as well as the rise of the Nazis to power in Germany in 1933. Industrial production, wages and tax revenue fell, while unemployment rose. In this difficult atmosphere, corruption scandals came to the fore, notably the Stavisky Affair, involving an embezzler with powerful political connections, of 1933–34. Fascistic movements exploited the situation, particularly the *Croix de feu*, which had 600,000 members by 1934. On 6 December, a violent demonstration created chaos in Paris. Austerity, meanwhile, won the government no support. In contrast, the blowing up in 1932 by Breton nationalists of a monument in Rennes to celebrate the Union of Brittany and France in 1532 was only a minor episode, as regionalism was not a major issue for France.

In response to the political crisis, the Left united in the *Front populaire* and won the May 1936 legislative elections. Léon Blum of the Socialists became prime minister. Among a string of Left-leaning initiatives, negotiations with major employers led to the Matignon Accords, which provided greater state and trade union roles in the economy; and a forty-hour working week was introduced along with two weeks' paid holidays, which was not the best way to compete with Germany. Wages rose but so did inflation. The railways were nationalized in 1937. However, exchange controls proved too much for the Senate, and this led to the fall of the government in June 1937. 'The wall of money' had allegedly defeated the government, an account that suited the myth of the Left, but, in practice, the Blum government was faced by a range of problems, including violent neo-fascists, notably the *La cagoule* movement, and, more seriously, like the Labour government in Britain in 1931, major divisions over what was practical in economic policy. The Popular Front dissolved in 1938 and the Left was not to return to power until 1981. Against a background of serious internal political divisions, the French government played a role in the appeasement of Germany and Italy in 1936–39, but moved towards hostility to further German expansion in 1939. This ensured that France went to war alongside Britain in September when Germany invaded Poland on 1 September 1939.

France by 1938 still had much in common with its earlier situation. With 35 per cent of employment in agriculture and a GDP per capita of $4,424, France was less 'modern' than the United States (18.5 per cent, $6,134), Britain (5 per cent, $5,983) and Germany (28.5 per cent, $5,126); although France imported less food than other major western European states. The French industrial sector was weaker than all three, and the number of patents filed lower. Although, in 1934, the Citroën car company had introduced the Traction Avant (the first mass-produced, front-wheel drive car), France, at 227,000 in 1938, ranked lowest of the four countries at car production, as well as in chemical production, although it was third in electricity production. The country was behind the USA, Germany and Britain in terms of investment, markets and industrial development, yet was still prosperous and productive. France also had the second largest empire in the world after Britain.

A greater level of national unity had been found in the adversity of war, which was followed by an entrenchment of central governmental intervention in many aspects of life. At the same time, political division came again to the fore in the late 1930s. The response to the Spanish Civil War (1936–39) had helped poison French politics and alarmists predicted the risk of a French civil war. In part, this was an aspect of the political divide that had begun with the French Revolution, one in which political, social, religious, cultural and local tensions and rivalries interacted. Thus, in crushing the Paris Commune in 1871, Adolphe Thiers wanted to show how a moderate leading a republic could subjugate the enemies of the bourgeoisie. The diversity of France, a country of pilgrimages that was also the capital of brothels, was a product of its variety, but also a source of great pressure.

11. The Second World War, 1939–1945

Politics is to the fore in the discussion of this period, as the Third Republic, discredited by defeat at the hands of Germany in 1940, was brought to an end that year by the collaborating Vichy regime. After the war came the Fourth Republic, its constitution backed by a referendum in 1946. In turn, and throwing light on the problems of devising a stable and successful political system, the difficulties of the Fourth Republic led to replacement in a peaceful quasi-coup by a more presidential Fifth Republic in 1958. None of this was apparent in 1940, as defeat brought occupation, collaboration and resistance, a result that reflected, but also exacerbated, existing political divisions.

Attacking on 10 May 1940, the Germans bypassed the fortifications of the Maginot Line, which guarded the eastern frontier further south and which can be approached today through the largely underground Fort de Fermont. Instead, advancing through the Ardennes and across the Meuse Valley at Sedan, the Germans broke through to the Channel near Abbeville. British and French forces to the north, which had advanced in order to prevent an anticipated German breakthrough on the Belgian plain, were cut off, and forced to evacuate via Dunkirk or to surrender. Having regrouped, the Germans then attacked the French to the south of the breakthrough zone, and after hard fighting on the rivers Marne and Somme, the outnumbered French broke, and the Germans entered an undefended Paris on 14 June.

The French had suffered from poor strategy, and weakness in air power and anti-tank guns, and from a failure to match the dynamic tempo of their German opponents. As a sign of a continued military determination, the French killed more Germans in June than in May, but they had lost cohesion as well as much equipment in the May fighting. Contributing to disorientation, there was also a massive flight of the population, known as the 'exodus' in what was called the 'Debacle': about seven million people, including about 60 per cent of the Parisian population, went west and south to escape the advancing Germans.

A political collapse played a crucial role. It was as if the High Command forgot its responsibilities in the face of defeat. The commander-in-chief, Maxime Weygand, was critical of the political system and pressing for an armistice, while Marshal Philippe Pétain, a deputy prime minister and hero of the First World War, was also pessimistic about the future and opposed to fighting on, which was the course urged by the British, most clearly Winston Churchill. Now based in Bordeaux, to where it had fled from Paris, the cabinet, on 15 June, agreed to find out the terms Germany would offer. On 16 June, Paul Reynaud, who wanted to fight on, resigned as prime minister, to be replaced by Pétain. The French asked for an armistice on 17 June, and accepted German terms on the 22nd, by which point German forces were in Nantes and Lyon, and advancing into southern France. At Hitler's insistence, the terms were signed in the railway carriage at Rethondes in which the Germans had accepted the armistice terms in 1918.

After the armistice, the French government left Bordeaux for Vichy, which was in the free zone that covered the south and part of central France, about 40 per cent of the country in total. The parts of Alsace and Lorraine gained by Germany in 1871 were annexed anew, while north and west France, including all the coastline – initially seen as the base area for an assault on Britain, providing invasion ports, airfields and naval bases – came under an occupation zone in which Vichy rule was under the German authorities. The airfields were the earliest to be developed, being used for example in the damaging raid on Coventry on 14–15 November 1940. By contrast, the submarine base at Saint-Nazaire was not completed until 1942, and still later had the roof heightened to its ultimate, and bombproof, form of nearly 8 metres (26 feet) of cleverly designed shock-dispersing layers. Notable remains include the formidable concrete submarine pens at Saint-Nazaire as well as at La Pallice (the deep-water port of La Rochelle). Subsequently, the coast was fortified to protect against Allied invasion. The Italians, who had attacked via an Alpine front on 10 June, but had scant success, made only limited territorial gains.

From their refuge in London, the Free French, under Brigadier-General Charles de Gaulle (1890–1970, see pl. XVIII), called for continued resistance but, although most of Equatorial Africa followed the Free French, much of the French empire came to follow orders from Vichy. In 1940–42, Vichy forces fought against British attacks with determination, notably at Dakar and in Lebanon, Syria and Madagascar, with Free French forces fighting alongside the British in the first three cases. The resistance at Dakar was successful, but the other places were conquered. However, Djibouti resisted a British blockade until December 1942 and Guadeloupe and Martinique held out until 1943.

In turn, Axis forces overran the Vichy zone without resistance from 10 November 1942. This was in response to Operation Torch, the Allied invasion of French North Africa, an invasion that had met only limited resistance two days earlier. However, the *ligne de démarcation* between Occupied France and Vichy France remained in force. The Italians used the opportunity to occupy a greater part of south-east France, in part reaching to the Rhône, although the Germans beat them to Marseille and Toulon, where, crucially, in the most important military act of resistance, the French warships were scuttled before the Germans could seize them. In September 1943, when Italy abandoned its German alliance, German forces occupied the Italian zone, with disastrous consequences for the many Jews who had fled there and for local Resistance groups that were now up against tougher opposition.

Within the Vichy elite, there was only limited support for fascism, as opposed to a more broadly-based conservative nationalism that was particularly open to Catholic activism. Yet, from the outset of Vichy France, there was a willingness to discriminate against Jews, and it did not require much German prompting, let alone pressure, to do so. The religious, cultural, political and social fault-lines of the Dreyfus Affair re-emerged as Vichy strove to create an ostentatiously Christian (especially Catholic) France. With the hostility to liberalism, communism, socialism, Freemasons, Jews and Protestants (although there were pro-Vichy Protestants) that was commonplace in Right-wing circles during the Third Republic, Vichy took forward the hostile conservative reaction to the Popular Front of the 1930s, and also drew on the *Action française*, notably the late 1930s anti-Semitic revival linked to opposition to Jewish refugees. Vichy presented the Third Republic, and particularly its politics, as decadent and weak, and in large part responsible for the defeat of 1940. Anti-British themes were emphasized, especially with a cult of Joan of Arc, who had been canonized in 1920, and the British invasion of Syria encouraged hostility, especially within the Vichy army. Vichy's account of the past was very much opposed to the French Revolution, especially its anti-Catholicism, and to Enlightenment figures such as the Abbé Grégoire who had pressed for equality, notably on behalf of Jews and slaves. The Germans destroyed his statue at Lunéville in 1942, while, under the Fifth Republic, the *Front national* was to attack his legacy.

At the same time, the need to respond to defeat and occupation, as well as other aspects of Vichy ideology, were in practice for some an excuse for collaboration with Germany as much as accommodation, and to a degree that can strike impartial observers as treasonable. Moreover, many who had made their names under the Third Republic proved all too willing to damn it, while benefiting from the misfortune of others. Thus, the philosopher Jean-Paul Sartre (1905–1980), who had fought in the French army and been made a prisoner-or-war, accepted a teaching post that was vacant because its Jewish holder had been removed. After the war, many French accommodators, and numerous collaborators, were able to pursue distinguished careers. Yet, there was also considerable complexity within Vichy as a result of strong cross currents. Conservative nationalism led to a hostility to German penetration, a hostility seen both in the hunting down of spies operating for the Germans, and in the determination to retain control of empire and fleet, keeping Germany as well as Britain at a distance. Yet, alongside the Vichy, but very different to its reactionary conservatism, there were fascist movements that propounded revolutionary ideas and competed with each other, the net effect being to increase Germany's options. In condemning the Third Republic and hailing the success of fascism elsewhere, the fascists looked to secure a place for France in Hitler's new order, which was not too different to the goal of Vichy, even if the latter was not fascist. The splintered character of the far-Right had weakened its pre-war influence, but it organized support for Pétain and its poisonous anti-Semitism flourished.

After 1940, the citizenship of many naturalized Jews was revoked by Vichy, and foreign Jews were interned, while there was legislation to define who were Jews and to exclude them from government posts including teaching. In 1941, there were further limitations on employment and commerce. In both the occupied and unoccupied zones, Jewish property was subject to confiscation, and the separate Police for Jewish Affairs was established by the Vichy Ministry of the Interior, measures intended to demonstrate a desire to cooperate with the Germans. In 1942, Vichy handed over foreign Jews for deportation to the concentration camps, and most of those deported that year were not under German control until handed over for movement out of the country. Vichy, however, was not so keen to hand over French Jews, in part because of a critical public reaction. In 1943, the deportations fell in number, and the roundups were mostly by the German *Schutzstaffel* (SS), and not the French police. The Vichy government knew that Jews were being sent to slaughter and fewer than 3 per cent of the 75,000 deported survived, in comparison to 59 per cent of the French non-Jews deported, mostly to the concentration camps at Ravensbrück and Buchenwald. In 1944, the *Milice*, a vicious security police established by Vichy in 1943, rounded up Jews. In total, nearly one-third of the Jews deported from France were French. For example, the Socialist former prime minister Léon Blum was arrested, tried for treason, and sent to imprisonment in concentration camps.

The public was split. Jews were protected especially in the Protestant-dominated Cévennes, and both Jewish compatriots and, albeit to a lesser extent, foreigners were helped on an individual level. The majority of French Jews, especially if children (some of whom were given over to adoption and brought up as Christians), survived the war. The percentage of survivors was far greater than in Belgium or the Netherlands. The Catholic Church included those willing to criticize the deportations, such as the Bishop of Montauban, and to take risks to help Jews, but there were also many others who preferred to accept, indeed support, Vichy, which also benefited from widespread anti-Semitism.

Although largely written out of the record, Vichy had much lasting influence (with legislation often simply renewed after 1944), and frequently unexpectedly so. For example, from 1943, the Institut national d'hygiène regularly collected data on cancer, and this led to the finalization of the nomenclature of cancers, which was important to the nomenclature adopted by the World Health Organization in 1952. A notion of stages of illness aided the classification system, and this notion shaped data on different lengths of survival, leading to the introduction in oncology of the idea of 'remission' in a schema until then restricted solely to 'curable' and 'incurable'. At the same time, the initial political context of Vichy's efforts was its determination to act in order to tackle demographic decline, a longstanding concern among French politicians. Vichy was very hostile to abortion, encouraged married women to stay at home and bear children, including by creating awards of medals for mothers with many children, and glorified Mother's Day celebrations. While continuing the Third Republic's natality programmes, this was now done in the name of 'travail, famille, patrie', which was the motto of the regime.

Aside from deliberate destruction, such as the dynamiting in January 1943 of the Old Port of Marseille by the French police as part of Hitler's 'purification' of the cosmopolitan city, France was heavily pillaged for the benefit of Germany, indeed greatly helping the latter maintain its war effort. The occupation costs in billions of francs rose from 81.6 in 1940, to 144.3 (1941), 156.7 (1942), 273.6 (1943) and 206.3 (1944); with the proportion of GDP being respectively 19.5, 36.8, 36.9, 55.5 and 27.9 per cent. A manipulated exchange rate also helped Germany control the economy. The mark-to-franc rate moved from one to eleven on 10 June 1940 to one to twenty on 25 June 1940. Food was purchased or requisitioned for the occupying forces, and also sent to Germany. As a result, daily calorie intake in France fell by a half, and there was serious malnutrition. The occupation of the so-called Free Zone (Vichy France) in November 1942 subsequently became harsher as a shortage of resources affected occupiers and the local population. Poverty helped ensure that some workers went voluntarily to work in Germany but compulsion as imposed by the Germans on Vichy in 1943 was the key element. In total about 646,000 civilians went to work there. In France, food shortages led to black-market activity and riots. Resistance activities became more intense, albeit being affected by the large-scale deportation of men for forced labour and by the harshness of German repression, which also benefited from support by collaborators.

Without suggesting any equivalence, the Vichy treatment of national history was to be paralleled by contentious post-war accounts of the war years, notably the role of the Resistance. There was no large-scale resistance in France after its rapid conquest in 1940. Instead, the Resistance, which was divided politically from the outset, took time to get going, as well as facing tensions, not least the determination of the de Gaulle government in exile to direct and represent it. The German invasion of the Soviet Union in June 1941 affected the views of French Communists: prior to that, the Soviet Union had been allied to Germany. In addition, the demands for forced labour in Germany encouraged Resistance recruitment, as did the awareness from the end of 1942 that the war was moving against the Axis. As a result, Resistance membership, which in 1941–42 had been hit very hard by German repression, rose greatly from early 1943, and became more significant militarily and politically from late 1943. Groups dedicated to sending intelligence, running escape lines and propaganda were increasingly supplemented by those prepared to take up arms. In part, this was due to the greater scale of the Resistance, but the establishment of the National Council of the Resistance under Jean Moulin in May 1943 was also important, not least to the struggle for legitimacy against Vichy.

The forces of the Maquis – a Corsican word for shrubland used to describe guerrilla bands of Resistance fighters – were armed by the British and were particularly strong in the Massif Central, Corsica, the Alps and Brittany. Resistance activity was affected by the terrain and natural cover, which helped explain there being more in the Massif Central than in the flat and well-cultivated Loire Valley. The discouraging nature of reprisals, especially the shooting of large (and totally disproportionate) numbers of civilians when German troops were killed, was also important. (Memorials to those killed, including street names, can be found across France.) A concern for the immediate needs of family and community, including food, discouraged resistance; and there was a willingness to negotiate relations with the occupiers, which was possible as long as armed resistance was avoided. Resistance activity was also affected by the detailed configurations of local politics and society, and their relationship with the complex dynamic of collaboration and resistance, a dynamic exploited by the Germans, the *Milice* and, in opposition, the Resistance. Few German soldiers were killed by the Resistance, but there was valuable intelligence gathering, acts of sabotage, help for escapees, and an important challenge to the position of Vichy.

A very different form of resistance was provided by the Free French forces, who played a major role from the outset, not least in the struggle over Vichy-run colonies, fighting in Gabon and Senegal in 1940 and Syria in 1941. In addition, the Free French took part in operations against German forces, as at Bir Hakeim in the battle of Gazala in Libya in the spring of 1942. This capability became more significant as a result of the conquest of French North Africa, which enabled a merger with the large French Army of Africa; and American-supplied equipment also helped greatly. Created in June 1943, the French Committee of National Liberation, which on 3 June 1944 became the Provisional

Government of the French Republic, provided a corps for the Allied conquest of Italy. This was followed by the provision of large forces in the reconquest of France in 1944, and notably so in southern France, especially in Operation Dragoon, the highly successful American–French invasion of Provence on 15 August. These forces then advanced into eastern France, where they fought the Germans in Alsace before advancing across the Rhine. The Free French lost about 3,200 in 1940–42 and the French Liberation Army in 1943–45 lost 25,730 with 75,823 wounded, with 1945 being the most deadly year for operations.

Within Occupied France, violence came to a height in the summer of 1944 as liberation appeared in prospect and the Germans responded to opposition with stark brutality. In the village of Oradour-sur-Glane near Limoges, 642 civilians were murdered by the Germans, with the men shot on sight and the women and children rounded up, locked in the local church and burned to death. Today the village stands as it was after the devastation, with the recent addition of the interactive Centre de la Mémoire. At Tulle, ninety-nine people were hanged by the Germans in June, while in June–July, the Germans brutally wiped out opposition on the Vercors plateau. On 14 July, a resistance group in Plumeliau, Brittany, was surrounded at dawn and sixty-two people were killed, and in the same sweep a group of fourteen was captured near Pontivy, tortured and soon after shot.

The withdrawal of the Germans from France in 1944 (which involved, in August, the Vichy government being moved to Germany) was an event celebrated across the country by the renaming of local squares as *Places de la Libération*. The celebrations were followed by a popular fury, called the *Épuration* (purge), directed against collaborators. Possibly up to 10,000 were killed and 40,000 detained. There was a harsh gender dimension, with many women who had had sex with Germans being publicly humiliated, notably by having their hair cut off and then being paraded in public. This fury was in part politically directed, but it also reflected the popular enmities that had built up under occupation, enmities that played a role in the texture of post-war politics, and notably so at the level of individual communities and families.

Subsequently there were trials for collaboration. The twenty-seven judicial district courts established by the Provisional Government charged 132,828 suspects between 1944 and 1948 with collaboration with the Germans or the *Milice*. Pétain, convicted of treason, was sentenced to death but the sentence was commuted to life imprisonment. Pierre Laval, the Vichy prime minister who was convicted of plotting against the security of the state and collaboration, was executed by firing squad.

The Provisional Government of the French Republic, declared in June 1944, replaced the French Committee of National Liberation, which had been created in June 1943. Keen to preserve sovereignty, de Gaulle was determined that France should not be put under Allied military occupation. A 'national unanimity' government was established on 9 September 1944, with the Communists and Socialists playing a major role in the government alongside the Popular Republican Movement led by Georges Bidault. Women and soldiers were granted the right to vote in 1944 (exercising it for the first time in 1945), and the Fourth Republic was established in 1946 as the result of deciding to abolish the Third.

Alongside the hatred between individuals and families that was left over from the occupation, there was an attempt to create an exemplary account of recent history, notably with an emphasis on the Resistance, although the Communist role in this was contested. This sanitization of the war years in terms of a myth of national resistance was to be given added force by the emphasis on de Gaulle during his presidency from 1958 to 1969. A workable past that greatly underplayed collaboration was constructed. This was seen as necessary in order to help rebuild national unity and confidence in the future.

The lives of those not involved directly in the fighting or sent to concentration camps were still devastated by the war as a result of German and Allied bombing: 12.6 per cent of the population was left homeless, and 45 per cent of the rail network was destroyed, including all the bridges downstream of Paris. The war cost about 150 per cent of GDP. Average daily calorie consumption, 2,830 in 1938, was 1,160 in 1946. Agricultural production did not really recover until 1948, and rationing ended the following year. GDP, $187 billion in 1938, was $102 billion in 1945, and still only $180 billion in 1948. Reconstruction took over twenty years.

Legacies of the war include German coastal defences, for example between Calais and the Somme estuary, and V-rocket launch sites, notably near Saint-Omer. There was particular devastation in the ports fortified and defended by the Germans, notably Brest, Dunkirk, Le Havre (which was over 80 per cent destroyed), Lorient and Saint-Malo, and as a result of the battle of Normandy, especially at Falaise and Saint-Lô. Air attacks caused much destruction, for example by the Germans on Abbeville in 1940 and Caen in 1944. Monuments of the occupation vary in their commemorative purpose. The Resistance is to the fore, as in the Mémorial du Mur des Fusillés in Arras (see pl. XIX), which refers to Resistance members shot by firing squad, and the prison gates at Saint-Lô. Museums include that of the Musée de la Résistance Bretonne at Saint-Marcel, where Resistance and Free French forces successfully engaged Germans in June 1944.

The Holocaust has been increasingly commemorated since the 1990s. The Natzweiler-Struthof concentration camp in Alsace and the Gurs internment camp near the Pyrenees, from which

Jews held in dire circumstances under the French administration were deported to the concentration camps, are particularly pointed reminders of the war. So too are the memorials, in almost every village and church, that record those killed in the conflict. What can be described as the German 'murder of the future' included shooting pupils who supported the Resistance, and those deaths are commemorated at the Collège Stanislas in Paris and elsewhere. The schools of that city also now bear plaques marking the seizure of Jewish pupils for slaughter.

12. France Reborn, 1945–1969

Rather than the Second World War, and the Fourth Republic to which it led, it was post-war economic and social transformation that was significant in resuming France's modernization and making it a different country. In what were subsequently called the *Trente Glorieuses* (Thirty Glorious Years), rapid economic development saw a major application of new technology, with significant mechanization, which led to a movement of people away from the land and to France becoming far less of a peasant society. Economic growth also encouraged immigration and, by 1973, the foreign workforce was 11 per cent, many of them from Spain, Portugal, Algeria, Vietnam and sub-Saharan Africa. This migrant flow was as important a social transformation of France as the cultural shift of the 1960s that more generally attracts attention.

Social change took a number of forms and drew on a range of interacting attitudes, so that consumerism was related to a more individual and independent attitude towards sex after the Second World War. At the same time, the political environment was significant because the fall of Vichy weakened what had become in wartime a heavy-handed Catholic moralism and altered the norms for wives and mothers. Children and young adults were given greater authority from the 1950s, and notably so young women, although there was much anxiety, and especially so over homosexuality.

There was also a change in France's economic position. Modernization of the economy required planned cooperation with West Germany in the key sectors of coal and steel, and the European Coal and Steel Community (ECSC) was agreed in the Treaty of Paris in 1951, which was followed by the establishment of the European Economic Community (EEC) in 1958. West German willingness to accept the concessions France required helped lead the latter to back the scheme. France wanted the ECSC and the EEC to help its modernization, but also to control West German independence, a goal justifying the loss of some national independence. The disastrous experience of the Second World War, which was underlined by the serious post-war failures in resisting insurgency in Indochina, from which France withdrew in 1954, and growing problems in Africa, lent energy to the idea of European union, as did the total failure of the Anglo-French Suez intervention in 1956, an intervention intended by France to resist Egyptian-backed Arab nationalism.

The fall and then removal of tariffs within the EEC led to a growth of trade, and, building on growth already in the 1950s, notably with consumerism and modernization, France had an average annual growth rate of 5.5 per cent in the first fifteen years of the EEC. To integrate, France had to dismantle a protectionist economic system and, in return, it insisted that the EEC adopt an agricultural system that served its farming interests, with the Common Agricultural Policy (CAP) finally agreed in 1960, after hard negotiations which provided for price guarantees and income support. This was an example of the way in which France successfully pressed for a form of European integration designed to advance its own interests. Within France, the CAP eased social tensions at a time of rapid agrarian change, but there was to be less concern for areas of heavy industry when they experienced even greater rates of decline later in the century.

Quarrels over the constitution of the new Fourth Republic had led to the resignation in January 1946 of Charles de Gaulle, who wanted a stronger executive, as head of the Provisional Government. The Left also lost traction in 1948 and a centrist politics came to the fore. However, as with the Third Republic, there was a major problem in ensuring ministerial stability, in part due to proportional representation, but even more so due to a lack of cooperation by centrist politicians, while major failures in colonial policy exacerbated the situation. Opposition movements included communism and, very differently, Poujadism, the latter a tax protest, led by the shopkeeper Pierre Poujade (1920–2003), that claimed to represent the ordinary French against the state, modernization and the elites. Poujade was a Vichy loyalist, although in 1942, after the German occupation of the 'free zone' of France, he joined the Resistance. He soon gained the nickname 'Poujadof', a reference to his huge public rallies of up to 200,000 people and his entourage of fascist sympathizers such as Jean-Marie Le Pen (b. 1928), later leader of the *Front national*, who shared Poujade's ardent determination to keep Algeria French. The anti-Semitism of the movement was directed in particular at Pierre Mendès-France, the Left-wing prime minister in 1954–55.

De Gaulle, as the unpopular Fourth Republic began to collapse in the context of a divided France, grasped power in 1958 and became prime minister. He presented a new constitution, establishing the Fifth Republic, in a speech to the nation delivered on 4 September. This was the anniversary of the proclamation of the Third Republic, and therefore an affirmation of continuity with the republican past, rather than, as his critics claimed, an authoritarian alternative. Nevertheless, the reduction in the power of the National Assembly also cut that of the political parties, whereas the president – the role to which de Gaulle was duly elected – who would chair the meetings of the Council of

Ministers, emerged as a key figure in a strengthened executive. This would give de Gaulle particular control over foreign policy. He was determined to reverse French decline, and to affirm and demonstrate national greatness.

To that end, in 1962, de Gaulle cut France free from its most onerous colonial commitment, that to Algeria, which rescued the state from a very heavy financial burden and the political system from the most divisive issue, one that was challenging its capacity to produce results. Two years earlier, most of French Africa had been granted independence, but that was not then regarded as an option for Algeria where there were many French settlers and which was administered as an integral part of France. However, in January 1961, a French referendum approved self-determination for Algeria. This was unwelcome to the European settlers there and to an important section of the army. In the face of the threat that a putsch in Algiers on 21–26 April 1961, by generals opposed to concessions, would spread to France, the government deployed tanks to protect the National Assembly and de Gaulle pointedly appeared on television in uniform. Control was maintained.

The following year, de Gaulle narrowly escaped an attempt to assassinate him by the *Organisation armée secrète* (OAS), an extremist terrorist group of European settlers. Algeria and mainland France witnessed terrorism by both the *Front de libé-ration nationale* (FLN), the indigenous Algerian movement, and the OAS, which notably carried out a bomb attack on the Paris–Strasbourg train on 18 June 1961. In addition, the state became more violent: on 17 October 1961, demonstrating Algerians were killed by the police in Paris. In 1962, terrorism intensified, but de Gaulle wanted to get rid of Algeria for more profound reasons, notably a sense that Algeria was a distraction from his mission to strengthen and modernize France and from the direction of his foreign policy. A referendum in France in

April 1962 on Algeria's independence led to an approval rate of
91 per cent. On 3 July, France recognized Algerian independence,
and on 22 August de Gaulle very narrowly survived another OAS
assassination attempt. European Algerians fled to France, as did
many of those who had worked with them.

Independence for Algeria enabled de Gaulle to consolidate
his position in France. The new political culture was demonstrated in October 1962 when, after his prime minister, Georges
Pompidou, was forced to resign by a motion of no confidence in
the National Assembly, de Gaulle immediately reappointed him.
Pompidou remained prime minister until 1968. De Gaulle's dissolution of the National Assembly after it passed, on 4 October
1962, a vote of censure against his proposal for the direct election
of the president, was also indicative of the new political culture.
On 28 October, he won support for the constitutional amendment
of a direct election for the president, rather than one chosen by the
National Assembly, by 62 per cent; while the elections of 18 and
25 November saw the Gaullists win a majority in the Assembly,
an unprecedented step for an individual party. De Gaulle's attitude
towards both the National Assembly and ministerial appoint-
ments reflected at once his autocratic manner and his rejection
of the political culture and structure of the Fourth Republic, a
rejection deliberately intended to achieve this authoritarian goal.
De Gaulle's family had a royalist background and he admired
Louis XIV, while the term Bonapartism was applied by his critics
(although that was a frequent criticism in French politics), notably
over the direct election.

De Gaulle, at the same time, benefited from the economic
growth and restructuring in France in the 1960s, and from the
ability to control inflation with the new franc introduced in 1960.
He did not care for economics, but understood the importance of
growth and was anxious to make sure that France modernized,

of which a clear sign was the commissioning in 1964 of France's first nuclear power station, at Avoine near Chinon. As earlier during the war, de Gaulle was not alone. He had competent people around him.

De Gaulle presented France as necessarily the leader of Europe, and this as a political and cultural dimension for France. The closer relationship with West Germany, seen with the Elysée Treaty of 1963, was matched by de Gaulle's determination to exclude Britain from Europe, as well as by his assault on American hegemony. He persuaded Konrad Adenauer, the West German chancellor, to reject the British idea, floated in 1957, of an International Free Trade Area, which answered British goals in Europe, not only in that the focus was on free trade, but also because Britain would have played an equal role in its formation. With the Fouchet Plan, pushed from 1961, de Gaulle envisaged a European Political Union, but in practice this French-dominated proposal, which failed because of opposition from the Netherlands, rested on de Gaulle's relationship with Adenauer. De Gaulle's rigid interpretation of French interests led to the Luxembourg compromise of 1965, under which an effective veto existed for member states in many fields of EEC activity, and no new states joined the EEC while de Gaulle, who was determined to see no dilution in his control, was president. With France now a nuclear power, he was also responsible for withdrawing France from NATO's integrated military command in 1966, as a result of which NATO's bases there closed.

Meanwhile, the Fifth Republic enjoyed considerable popularity within France, in part because the Fourth had provided no stability but also due to the divisions elsewhere on the political spectrum. However, as a reminder of the role of contingency, de Gaulle failed to win an overall majority in the first round of the presidential elections held in 1965, and was forced into a second-round run-off with the Socialist François Mitterrand, in which de Gaulle won with only 55.2 per cent of the votes cast. Moreover, in the first ballot of the National Assembly elections held in 1967, the Gaullists and their allies gained only 38 per cent of the vote.

An alternative route to power for the Left was suggested by a major upsurge in radical action. Students moved to the Left, a Left not of communism but of a direct action through Maoism (modelled on the Revolutionary Guards of Mao Zedong's China) and anarchism. Student activism in 1967 was followed in May 1968 by demonstrations and violence in Paris and other cities (see pl. XXII). A brutal response by the riot police in Paris led to a consolidation of support around the students, including a general strike followed by more sustained trade-union action and political pressure from the Left for governmental change. Assured on 29 May, as a result of a visit to the commanders of the French forces in West Germany, of military support if necessary, de Gaulle showed determination in a radio broadcast on 30 May, and regained the initiative, encouraged by a mass demonstration that day by his supporters in Paris. On 23 and 30 June, ably organized by Pompidou, de Gaulle's followers won an overwhelming majority in legislative elections, while the Left did badly. The student movement collapsed due to its divisions, as well as to a fall in worker and popular support.

De Gaulle resigned less than a year later, on 28 April 1969, after the government lost a referendum on relatively minor constitutional changes with reference to the composition of the Senate and a move from *départements* to regions. The referendum was understood to be in part about de Gaulle's continuance in office. He had divided the Right with his proposals, while inflation was hitting much of the public. Fifty-three per cent voted no. This was a fizzling out, like that of Margaret Thatcher in Britain in 1990, not that either would have appreciated the comparison. De Gaulle died on 9 November 1970.

Culturally, France was most significant in these years for writing and cinema, notably the *Nouvelle Vague* (New Wave) of the late 1950s, with films that contrasted with those of Hollywood in accepting the complexity of life. There was a parallel to student radicalism in the scrutiny and criticism of authority by intellectuals such as Michel Foucault, who presented information as being employed by the state in order to cement control. At the same time, the variety of French thought included *L'énergie humaine* and *Le phénomène humain* by the Jesuit geologist and philosopher Pierre Teilhard de Chardin (1881–1955), who described humans as evolving towards a perfect spiritual state, but fell foul of the Catholic Church, which refused to grant permission for publication. The ecumenical community at Taizé, founded in 1940, serves as another reminder of the variety of Christian thought and activity.

Meanwhile, there had been much building and rebuilding, as war damage was replaced, urbanization catered for, and much of the housing modernized. Many of the works of the period had scant architectural distinction, but they can be found across France. The transformation of the economy in the 1950s and, even more so the 1960s, saw a major growth in the middle class while, alongside pronounced, indeed growing, inequality, the working class benefited from rising income and low unemployment. Much of this wealth was spent on consumer goods, notably cars, but also white goods, such as refrigerators, while telephone use increased. Consumer industries grew, while heavy industry and mining declined, as did agricultural employment. As elsewhere in the West, a baby boom, which in France had begun in 1942 in part because of pro-birth policies, was another expression of consumerism, and contrasted greatly with lower birth rates earlier in the century.

13. Modern France, 1969–2000

Having seen off the challenge of 1968, conservatives dominated France in the 1970s, first under Georges Pompidou (1911–1974), who won the presidency in 1969 with 57.6 per cent of the vote, and then, after his death in office, under Valéry Giscard d'Estaing (b. 1926), who beat the Socialist Mitterrand with 50.8 per cent of the votes cast and retained the presidency until 1981. The position of the Right was challenged, however, by the more general economic turmoil of the 1970s. The global economic crisis of 1973 was followed in France, from 1975, by lower average annual rates in GDP as well as in wages, and by a rise in unemployment. During the Giscard presidency, after the more protectionist, Gaullist Jacques Chirac (1932–2019) had resigned as prime minister, the government of the highly intelligent Raymond Barre (1924–2007), a former economics professor who was prime minister from 1976 to 1981, responded with economic liberalization, cutting the government's role and emphasizing market forces, not least in putting control of inflation above unemployment. Barre removed most price controls, enabling public services, such as the railways, to raise their prices and cost the state less, and also cut down on the industrial aid designed to maintain employment, an austerity measure that made him very unpopular. These policies were part of the opening up of the economy to outside influences, which brought growth, but also problems, and Barre's unpopularity indicated the difficulty of this shift away from state control and direction.

Reducing industrial assistance was more controversial than removing price controls (although the two were linked through encouraging competitiveness), because the former had immediate implications for unemployment, which rose to one million in 1977, implications seen in 1979 with the crisis in the steel industry that was central to the traditional economy in Lorraine. Barre pressed for a reduction in capacity that entailed the laying off of 20,000 workers, but this policy led to mass agitation there, and he had to back down and provide more state money: in the French fashion, of *capitalisme d'état* (state capitalism), Barre's conservatism was more *dirigiste* and top-down than that of Margaret Thatcher (1925–2013), prime minister of Britain during the 1980s.

In 1981, there was a major break, apparently political, economic and cultural, when Giscard was replaced by the Socialist candidate, François Mitterrand (1916–1996). Opponents covered the eyes of Giscard on his electoral posters with cut-out paper diamonds, representing the precious stones he had allegedly received from 'Emperor' Jean-Bédel Bokassa, the brutal dictator of the Central African Republic from 1966 to 1979, and also the sense of corruption associated with both the President and the old order. The story circulated of Giscard attempting to show his popularity by taking the *métro*, only for it to be revealed before the attendant journalists that he did not know how to buy a ticket. The Right was divided in the election campaign between Giscard and Chirac, who had relaunched the Gaullist movement as the *Rassemblement pour la République* (Rally for the Republic) in 1976, and who became mayor of Paris in 1977 when, under a law of 1975, the mayoralty was re-established in place of the city being under the control of a prefect. The two men won more votes in the first round of the 1981 election than Mitterrand and the unreconstructed Communist Georges Marchais, but, in the run-off between the two leading candidates, Mitterrand benefited from a consolidation on the Left that was lacking on the Right, where about a sixth of those who had voted for Chirac now did so for Mitterrand, who won 51.75 per cent of the vote.

The latter's victory was presented as the *grand soir* that would usher in a new political age, and with a reference to the past that typified a longstanding feature of part of the political debate, *Le Monde* greeted the result: 'the Bastille falls again'. Large numbers of Mitterrand's supporters flocked to public places to celebrate. Mitterrand then called legislative elections in which the Socialists, having raised the minimum wage, family allowances and low-income housing subsidies, won a majority in the National Assembly: 283 out of 491 seats. There was now no need for an alliance with the Communists, although they were included in the government, while the Right was clearly defeated. Liberal measures introduced by the new government included, in 1981, the abolition of the death penalty, the loosening of immigration regulations, and the decriminalization of homosexual acts, each a major change to the Catholic code. Euphoria, however, led to a wave of unrealistic hopes about radical transformation through state-driven change. More positively, the Fifth Republic in 1981 had displayed a sophistication and stability capable of accepting an alternation between Right and Left.

In many respects, the policies subsequently followed in 1981–83 linked the traditional nostrums of the Left and of state control and intervention, albeit, in 1982, with the addition of the decentralization of powers from prefects to the regional councils. Barre's unpopularity confirmed the Socialists in their determination to use state subsidies to maintain employment, and reflation focused less on modernization than on support for historic industries – coal, steel and shipbuilding; while a determined effort was made to control manufacturing and the financial system. There were large-scale nationalizations in 1982, as well as exchange controls

Map 79

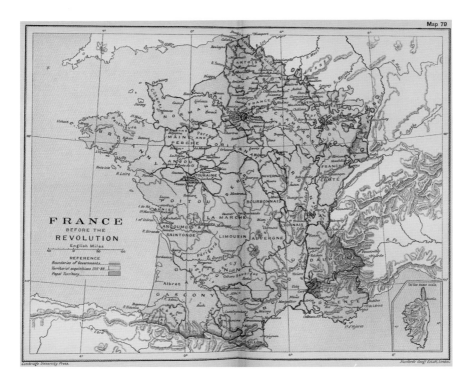

Map 103

XII & XIII, PREVIOUS PAGE Two contemporary maps clearly illustrate the changes in French territory before and after the turmoil of the Revolution.

XIV, ABOVE *Barricades de la Commune, avril 71. Coin de la place Hotel de Ville & de la rue de Rivoli*, Pierre-Ambrose Richebourg, 1871.

XV, OPPOSITE Sacré-Coeur was the most dramatic instance of the Culture Wars of the late nineteenth century, a key affirmation of Church power.

LE PROCÈS DE RENNES
Dreyfus amené au Conseil de guerre

XVI, OPPOSITE *The Call to Arms*, Auguste Rodin, 1879. The arts were ably deployed in the cause of a new Republican ideology.

XVII, ABOVE *Dreyfus being retried at Rennes*, 1899. The trial transfixed and divided France.

XVIII, TOP Keeping the flame alive: General de Gaulle in exile during the Second World War saluting Free French commando troops in London in 1942 on Bastille Day.

XIX, ABOVE Memorial plaques to commemorate over 200 Resistance fighters executed in the citadel in Arras. The Germans fought the Resistance with great brutality.

XX, TOP An image of a passing France. Blue Citroen 2CV parked outside a bakery in Limoges, 2011. Now, the supermarket has taken over.

XXI, ABOVE The Tour de France. An annual epic that passes by at an amazing speed. The peloton in the mountains during the 105th Tour de France 2018, Stage 19 from Lourdes to Laruns.

XXII, TOP Riots in the Latin Quarter in Paris, May 1968. A crisis of power and governance that caused de Gaulle to waver for a moment.

XXIII, ABOVE Riot in Paris by the *gilets jaunes* (yellow vests), 2019. A slow-moving challenge to the authority of the Macron presidency that for some also called into question the logic of its modernizing purpose.

in a futile attempt to prevent capital flight and to protect the franc. Taxation was directed towards redistribution, with a wealth tax matched by an increase in the minimum wage, a cut in the working week and a reduction in the retirement age.

This policy rested in part on a refusal to accept the disciplines posed by international economic competition; indeed, on their rejection as alien Anglo-American concepts. Mitterrand's ambitious policies, supported by Pierre Mauroy (1928–2013), prime minister between 1981 and 1984, were rapidly thwarted, however, by economic realities and the disciplines of the EEC, as a one-country siege economy was not possible, not least because it was unacceptable to West Germany where the Right-wing Christian Democrats gained power in 1982. There were also signs of serious tensions within France itself as inflation and unemployment rose. Strikes, notably in 1983, and demonstrations were accompanied by a business crisis, by pressure on the franc within the European monetary system, and by a large-scale movement of currency abroad. Meanwhile, working-class disenchantment with the government grew along with the determination of trade unions to secure guarantees for their members on pay, pensions and conditions.

This situation encouraged Mitterrand to decide on a reversal of policy from June 1982, although, typically, he only committed himself after the Socialists did badly in the municipal elections on 6 and 13 March 1983. Elements of the Barre policy were reintroduced, not least a struggle against the inflation which hit business confidence and challenged the value of money, and thus the established social order, while public spending, which had risen greatly in 1981, was cut. A distinctive French path to socialism was no longer the goal or rhetoric of policy, and, instead, Mitterrand broke with the Left and pressed for a 'mixed' economy. Now very unpopular, Mauroy resigned as prime minister in June 1984, being replaced by the technocrat Laurent Fabius (b. 1946) from 1984 to

1986, a self-conscious modernizer who sought to help private business and consciously presented himself as breaking from socialist orthodoxies.

Cultural conservatism, meanwhile, was marked with major demonstrations against the government's attempt to cut subsidies to private Catholic schools, which was correctly seen as motivated by a desire for secularization, and, on 24 June 1984, led by Chirac, the mayor, a million people marched in Paris against the legislation. Mitterrand had already announced its withdrawal on television. Such demonstrations, however, tend to be ignored in a narrative of protest focused on radical politics. The 1984 demonstrators' emphasis on the value of religion contrasted with the stress on toleration, the Renaissance and the Enlightenment – what Jack Lang, the Socialist Minister of Culture for most of the period 1981–93, called 'Europe's soul'. This contrast was an aspect of a longstanding culture war, one refocused, in the context of rising unemployment (2.5 million by 1986), by increased opposition to immigration, and notably from North Africa. The *Front national* won the town of Dreux in the municipal elections of 1983 and, by exploiting immigration as a political issue, made a wider breakthrough across France. Mitterrand wanted to break the Right by using the extreme Right against it, and in the process instrumentalized the immigration problem.

Meanwhile, there were debates about the reading of French history. Communist scholars, such as the influential Albert Soboul, professor at the Sorbonne from 1966 to 1982, were keen advocates of a Marxist interpretation of the Revolution, seeing it as a bourgeois victory over, first, the old order of the *ancien régime* and, then, popular radicalism. In contrast, revisionists, such as François Furet in his *Penser la Révolution française* (1978), contested this interpretation, both by challenging the Marxist thesis and by pressing the need to move away from a socio-economic account of the Revolution. In practice, however, the impact of the Right in the universities remained slight.

The National Assembly elections of 1986 were won by the Right and Chirac became prime minister, launching a 'cohabitation' with Mitterrand that lasted until 1988. The new government was tougher on immigration, but faced a challenge from strikes as well as from terrorism, notably from the radical Left-wing *Action directe*. Inflation was brought under control, but unemployment remained high. Nevertheless, Mitterrand was able to appear above politics as '*la force tranquille*' (quiet strength). The energy of the Left was strengthened in 1988 when Mitterrand was re-elected president, defeating Chirac, in the second round on 8 May, with 54 per cent of the vote. Yet again, divisions among the non-Left proved crucial: Barre, the candidate for the centre, had been eliminated in the first round, as had Jean-Marie Le Pen of the *Front national*, who came fourth with 14.4 per cent. Mitterrand was helped by the decline of the Communist Party. Moreover, the victory of the Right under Chirac in the National Assembly elections in 1986 was reversed in 1988 with new elections. Michel Rocard, the Socialist most acceptable to non-Socialists, became prime minister, but was to be forced to resign in 1991, which was a victory for Mitterrand's characteristic ability to manipulate proceedings. As an instance of the latter, he had altered the electoral system in order to increase the challenge to the Right's established party from the *Front national*. However, in March 1993, the Socialists were badly beaten in the legislative elections, and another period of cohabitation began.

Allegedly remarking, 'I will be the last great president', Mitterrand had a sense of grandeur. When I encountered him in 1989 during the Revolution bicentennial he struck me as a would-be personification of history: the closest I was going to get to seeing Louis XIV in action. Although his style was very eclectic, under

Mitterrand the very expensive *grands projets*, such as the 'People's Opera' at the Bastille, the new National Library and the Grande Arche at La Défense, were presented as a justification of the government and as an opportunity to advance its views. Containing an exhibition centre as well as a library, the Grande Arche, finished in 1989, was described as a modern equivalent to the Arc de Triomphe, one focused on humanitarian ideals and not war. In 1995, speaking to the European Parliament, Mitterrand disparaged nationalism as bellicose, and he presented his European policy accordingly as benign, but, in practice, like other French leaders, he very much advanced a French interpretation of Europe, and understandably so.

Mitterrand was embroiled in the history wars about Vichy that became increasingly prominent from the 1980s. Aside from an ambivalent war record and a seemingly manufactured assassination attempt in 1959, he proved a particularly ambiguous figure, adamantly refusing to apologize for the Vichy regime, being a friend to Vichy figures and sending wreaths to Pétain's tomb. One of Mitterrand's friends, René Bousquet, wartime chief of police in the Occupied Zone, had allowed the use of police in arresting Jews and had pressed for the deportation of foreign Jews to eastern Europe. Bousquet was assassinated in 1993, just before he could be tried for his role in rounding up Jewish children for deportation to slaughter. Maurice Papon, the wartime secretary-general at the Prefecture of the Gironde, who had played a major role in the deportation of Bordeaux's Jews before having a distinguished post-war career as a minister and official, was only arrested after Mitterrand's death. While in line with earlier cover ups, Mitterrand's stance was increasingly out of keeping with a culture of openness that was slowly developing. In contrast to Mitterrand and to the use of Vichyist themes by the *Front national*, Chirac in 1995 accepted national responsibility for the wartime treatment of Jews.

The sickly Mitterrand did not stand for a third term in 1995. The first round was won by the Socialist candidate Lionel Jospin, but Chirac won the run-off, benefiting from a consolidation on the Right. The need to reduce government expenditure, an issue Mitterrand had never taken seriously, led Alain Juppé, the prime minister appointed by Chirac, to propose cuts in expenditure, but these resulted in mass demonstrations and helped in 1997 to lead to the defeat of his government at the election. The *Financial Times* had warned on 9 May:

> While the right is making no bones of the need for further medicine to give the economy more *élan*, the left is still talking the cushy language of state-created jobs and shorter working hours….a victory for the right…is most likely….But…it is difficult to believe such a weakened government would have much appetite remaining to support investor-friendly restructuring of French industry.

Defeat forced Chirac back to 'cohabitation' with the Socialists, with Jospin becoming prime minister. The system did not work well, and that problem exacerbated Chirac's preference for gesture politics, especially in foreign policy, rather than for addressing systemic problems in the economy. In a search for popularity, and as a misleading way to address unemployment, the Socialist government capped weekly working hours at thirty-five hours in 2000–2, a rigid provision that harmed productivity.

Alongside partisan strife, there was political management by an 'alite'. The graduates of the *grandes écoles*, especially the École Polytechnique and the École Nationale d'Administration (ENA), established in 1945 to provide meritocratic leadership, dominated government, politics and business through a nepotistic system called *pantouflage*, and provided continuity accordingly.

Giscard, Chirac, Rocard, Jospin, Juppé, Dominique de Villepin and Emmanuel Macron were all ENA graduates. The more widespread democratic deficit was seen when the Juppé government introduced the measures intended to cut government spending by decree, and not via the National Assembly where they would face criticism.

THE FOOTBALL WORLD CUP of 1998 was held in France, with the final played at the newly commissioned Stade de France in Saint-Denis, north Paris. The location of the new national stadium in that multicultural suburb was no accident. The team reflected a very modern, diverse France, drawing on an ethnically diverse group of players with backgrounds from West and North Africa, the Caribbean, Pacific islands, Armenia, the Basque Country and elsewhere. France had never won the World Cup before, so the 'Rainbow' team's victory in the final became a watershed moment for the nation and a strong unifying force both domestically and internationally. The final cemented a period of French domination of football, as they went on to win the following European Championship, and it launched the international careers of a generation of great footballers.

Meanwhile, economic and social change transformed much of France's life and culture, even though tourists tended not to notice this. Transformation was readily apparent in the infrastructure, notably with improved communication routes and the spread of nuclear power. The views of local communities, as well as traditional patterns of spatial organization, were very much subordinated in the planning process for high-speed rail networks, and the concerns communities voiced about disruption had scant impact on the routing. The first line of the prestigious high-speed train TGV (*train à grande vitesse*), travelling at 270 kph (168 mph), opened between Paris and Lyon in 1981–83, and bypassed Dijon, a longstanding rail hub that was thereby marginalized. A TGV line to Brittany had opened by 1990, Marseille following in 2001 and Strasbourg in 2016. The expanding *autoroute* system also bypassed former centres on the *routes nationales*, as did the building of major bridges, such as the Pont de Normandie (1995) across the Seine from Le Havre to Honfleur. Traffic therefore did not have to cross middle-sized cities such as Rouen. Large-scale coastal resorts were another change, springing up as on the Languedoc coast or at La Baule in Brittany. The TGV stations were an aspect of the functionalism of the period that proved compatible with an exciting architectural language. Other aspects of culture remained vibrant, including cinema and the arts, the latter focused by the Musée National d'Art Moderne in Paris's Pompidou Centre, which had opened in 1977.

Change could also involve a desire for preservation, as with the rise of environmentalism as an issue. Although the word *environnement* only came into common usage in the 1980s, the Ministry for the Protection of Nature and the Environment was established in 1971. In part, environmentalism drew on the counter-culture of 1968 and its critique of industrial capitalism, and in part on older ruralist currents. One product of the latter was a rural protectionism against development expressed in part by support for the Common Agricultural Policy, but, more pointedly, by the creation of national parks, such as those in the Pyrenees in 1967 and the Cévennes in 1970, and regional ones, such as that in the Landes region in south-western France in 1970.

Meanwhile, there was a hollowing out of parts of rural France, in part as a result of the very European project that Mitterrand endorsed, in particular the admission of Spain into the European Economic Community in 1986. This challenged agriculture in southern France, and notably, but not only, the production of wine and fruit. In response, French farmers seized lorries carrying Spanish produce and destroyed the loads. These actions reflected an underlying malaise in which a traditional way of life was being hit hard by change, not least the process later disparaged as globalization but more realistically a matter of competition both within France and in the EU. The south was hit particularly hard, but there was also serious competition where the soil was poor, as in Brittany. The major significance of the countryside in French ideas of identity underlined the severity of the crisis, but there were also problems in urban areas, with traditionally male blue-collar jobs going, while many of the new ones in the service sector were filled by women.

14. France Today, 2001–

The tensions, if not the precariousness, of national democracy were indicated by the presidential elections of 21 April and 5 May 2002. In the first round, and benefiting from a focus on North Africans living in France and fears of unemployment and crime, Jean-Marie Le Pen (b. 1928), the candidate of the far-Right *Front national*, who had been accused of perpetrating torture during the Algerian War, received more votes than the Socialist candidate, Lionel Jospin, who had served as prime minister since 1997, a reversal of their results in that year. Jospin was beleaguered by a serious lack of personal charisma, divisions on the Left, including within the fratricidal Socialists, and the unpopularity of the government. Amidst misleading talk of the rise of fascism, there was a second-round run-off between Le Pen and Chirac. The latter won handsomely by 82 to 18 per cent, benefiting from the determination across the political spectrum, including on the Left, to defeat Le Pen, and acknowledging this by saying that he understood that many people would be lending him their vote. Victory for Chirac provided him with an opportunity to bring cohabitation with the Socialists to an end, and the legislative elections of June saw a strong victory for him.

Alongside high productivity in the private sector, the economic situation remained an issue, not least when growth declined in 2001–2. By the second quarter of 2005, French unemployment was at 10 per cent, compared to 5.5 per cent in the United States, and youth unemployment, at over 23 per cent, was far higher.

Government debt rose, although, in January 2008, the fall of sterling against the euro helped ensure that France replaced Britain as the world's fifth largest economy. In a referendum in May 2005, the French rejected the draft European constitution by 55 per cent, with the Left and the *Front national* being especially opposed, and the free movement of workers and jobs particularly unpopular. Meanwhile, Chirac had stayed out of the 2003 Iraq War, thus demonstrating national independence from the United States, affirming links with similarly neutral Germany and avoiding the burdens of war.

The Chirac years came to an end in 2007 with a combination of political impasse and a high level of suspicion about political ethics that involved both Chirac and his prime minister, and destined successor, Dominique de Villepin. Indeed, that year, Chirac was formally charged by magistrates with embezzlement while mayor of Paris, a position he held from 1977 to 1995. Outmanoeuvring Villepin to become the candidate of the Right, Chirac's successor, Nicolas Sarkozy (b. 1955), who had been an anti-Islamicist interior and finance minister under Chirac, in part campaigned for the presidency as an outsider to the mores of the Chirac years and, linked to that, promised a break with the past. Riots in the poor, immigrant-dense suburbs of Paris in October–November 2005, which featured the torching of thousands of cars, provided Sarkozy with an opportunity to appear tough. His criticism of the supposed role of immigration and Islamism was countered by arguments that social exclusion, and the resulting very high rate of youth unemployment, were key issues, but the criticism hit hard and Sarkozy's popularity rose. The government sought to address the latter in 2006 by reducing employment protection for those under twenty-six, and thus encouraging hiring, but this measure led to a mass demonstration on 18 March 2007 and such pressure resulted in the government rescinding the legislation.

In the 2006–7 presidential campaign, Ségolène Royal (b. 1953) won the Socialist primary, while Sarkozy, with his emphasis on a 'crisis of identity' and his promise to establish a 'Ministry of Immigration and of National Identity', dominated the Right. On 22 April 2007, he topped the poll with 30.6 per cent, compared to Royal's 25.7 per cent and Le Pen's mere 10.4 per cent. Royal did well in the south-west and the Massif Central, traditional Left-wing areas under the Third Republic. In the second round, Sarkozy won with 53 per cent, attracting votes from both the poor and the rich, before going on to win the legislative elections.

In 2005, when Chirac forced the European Commission to back down over its plan to open the European Union's (EU) market in services, the Fraser Institute's Economic Freedom of the World Index had Britain tied for fifth place, Germany eighteenth and France fifty-second. There was a measure of economic liberalization in the late 2000s, notably tax cuts in 2007 and the restructuring of the hospital system in 2009, while television channels were allowed to earn money through product placement from 2010. Economic nationalism continued: in 2007, a foreign takeover of the natural gas company *Gaz de France* was blocked, and, in 2008, there was hostility to any foreign takeover of the poorly managed bank *Société Générale*. With his conviction of the value of the state, Sarkozy was less of an Anglo-American style neoliberal than his critics claimed, a contrast more generally true of French politicians on the Right. At the same time, as an aspect of liberalization, French companies invested abroad, Renault building its successful Laguna car in Romania, where in 1999 it had taken over Dacia, creating a number of affordable models to supplement the Renault range.

As with earlier attempts at reform during the Chirac presidencies, reforms under Sarkozy led to opposition in the form of strikes. Sarkozy initially proved more robust than Chirac, who was prone to turn back in the face of demonstrations, notably in

1995. The contrast between the 2007 transport strikes and earlier action suggested strikes had less impact in part because public-service unions had become less important, while society's increased complexity meant a greater unwillingness to think in terms of a Marxist clash between social blocs. Communism had declined in France as an attitude, a tendency and a party, and far-Left trade unions had relatively few members, although this minority continues to exert disproportionate political pressure.

Nevertheless, the success of the Socialists in municipal elections in March 2008 revealed that the Sarkozy honeymoon had been very short term. France was hit hard by the global recession of 2008 and also by opposition to his personal life, attitudes and ostentation, and the regional elections in March 2010 were dire. The government's attempts to handle pension issues in order to address the deficit proved more damaging than attempts to raise popularity by adopting an anti-Muslim line as well as increasing taxes on the wealthy. The *Front national* became more challenging.

Sarkozy lost the 2012 election, held on 22 April and 6 May, by 48.4 per cent to 51.6 per cent to François Hollande (b. 1954), the Socialist candidate. Marine Le Pen (b. 1968), who had succeeded her father as head of the *Front national* in 2011, came third with 17.9 per cent of the first ballot. In the legislative elections held in June, the Socialists won a majority. However, Hollande proved the most unpopular president of the Fifth Republic as economic issues, notably high unemployment, contributed to an abiding sense of malaise that Hollande's reforms could not shift. The Left were angered by what they saw as his neoliberalism, austerity and maintenance of Sarkozy's immigration policies; and liberalization, in the shape of the legislation of homosexual marriage (2013) and of the regulations on abortion (2013, 2016), did not alter that situation. Continued pressure from the *Front national*, notably in the municipal elections of March 2014, the European ones of May

2014 and the regional ones in December 2015, increased tension on the Left, which had no effective response to the fall in GDP and employment. Accusations of corruption became an issue, while Hollande's busy personal life compounded his problems and made him seem ridiculous to some.

Hollande was also affected by concern about Islamic radicalism, concern exploited by Marine Le Pen, who faced charges in early 2014 for comparing the spill-over of Islamic prayers into the streets to a Nazi occupation. Her stance, however, implicitly criticized Vichy, an approach which disassociated herself from her father's favour for Vichy and his identification with anti-Semitism, and a rift between the two became public in 2014. Islamist terrorist attacks on Paris in January 2015, *Charlie Hebdo* on 13 November 2015 and Nice on 14 July 2016 led to a robust government response with the deployment of troops in the major cities. These attacks shook France, so often used to seeing terrorism as imported, as most of the perpetrators were born in France or elsewhere in Europe.

Some of the criticism of Hollande was distinctly overblown, as in 2012 when Boris Johnson, then mayor of London, compared Hollande's ministers to the radical and violent *sans-culottes* of the Revolution. So also in 2014, with the dispute over the Hollande government's attempt to revise terminology and laws in order to ensure legal parity between men and women. The Right, in response, evoked a range of references, not only Orwellian language, but also the attempts of the Revolutionaries to transform French society in the 1790s. Najat Vallaud-Belkacem, the minister for women's rights, was dubbed an indefatigable Fouquier-Tinville of familial practices and personal habits, a reference to the public prosecutor during the Terror. The government backed down, as it had done the previous year when a new eco tax, a charge on large trucks using main roads in a 'green' effort to discourage road freight, led in Brittany to large-scale demonstrations as well as to attacks on toll sensors. The demonstrators waved Breton flags and wore *bonnets rouges*, an echo of the headgear worn in a 1675 Breton rising against taxes imposed by Louis XIV.

Hollande's clear and consistent unpopularity ensured that he did not stand for re-election in 2017 but, in the campaign, the Left was divided while the conventional Right in the person of its candidate, François Fillon, was hit by corruption charges. The run-off in the election on 7 May, under martial law – an unprecedented situation due to the *Charlie Hebdo* terrorist attack of 2015 – was between Emmanuel Macron of the new *La République en marche* party and Marine Le Pen. Even though the first ballot was close, with Le Pen winning almost 22 per cent, Macron won on the second ballot by 66 to 34 per cent. Macron (b. 1977), the youngest head of state of the Fifth Republic and the second youngest head of state in modern French history, only Napoleon Bonaparte being younger, went on to win the legislative elections that followed. Again, Macron benefited from there being no real opposition.

Earlier a member of Hollande's government, Macron presented himself as a centrist reformer, and his policies and stance led to opposition. The *gilets jaunes* (yellow vests) protests, which began in November 2018, included a blockade of fuel depots and had begun against fuel taxes and the cost of living (see pl. XXIII). The protests were grounded in displeasure not only at the role of government in terms of policy issues – notably over taxation, including the scrapping of the wealth tax alongside a tax rise on fuel – but also on Macron personally, as there was the widespread sense of the President not caring about the people. In December 2019, Macron's attempt to reform the very expensive pension provisions led to the Communist-aligned CGT Labour Federation to call a strike. Macron also found terrorism a challenge.

Alongside politics and government as matters of policy and probity, the underside of corruption continued to play a role in the early twenty-first century. The personal life of presidents attracted attention, but the interplay of power with business interests, both licit and illegal, was more striking. There could be the mentality of the witch-hunt, as in Toulouse in 2003 when, in the *seconde affaire Alègre*, there were accusations of sado-masochistic orgies linking magistrates and the police to pimps, prostitutes and drugs, with murder, rape, torture and corruption allegedly part of the brew. Such paranoid fantasies were far from new, but they reflected a social uneasiness about sex and power that lent itself to personal antagonism and media campaigns. More mundanely, there were financial scandals. Pierre Bérégovoy, the recently defeated Socialist prime minister, committed suicide in 1993 while facing investigation concerning a large interest-free loan he had received. Alain Juppé, prime minister from 1995 to 1997, was convicted of corruption in 2004, while Dominique de Villepin was charged in 2007 with falsely claiming, in the 'Clearstream affair', that his then ministerial rival, Sarkozy, had profited from an arms deal. In 2020, Sarkozy was put on trial on corruption charges, accused of trying to obtain classified information from a judge. Corruption played a major role in French crime thrillers, for example *Engrenages* (Spiral), a continuing television police procedural set in Paris of which the first series was shown from December 2005.

There were also more systemic links, such as the longstanding one between the government, the oil giant Elf-Aquitaine and the oil-producing states in which it operated, particularly Angola and Gabon, links that provided an opportunity to avoid dependence on non-French oil companies. In addition, the web of corruption entailed secret funds that washed around French politics and business, and, in 2002, funded an unsuccessful attempt by Charles Pasqua, a robust Gaullist, to seek the presidency, while, in the 1990s, Elf was party to the slush-fund scandal that linked Mitterrand to Helmut Kohl, the German chancellor.

At the same time as political instability, France was affected by general environmental changes. For example, in 2003, 14,000 people died prematurely due to a prolonged heatwave, while, in 2005–6, water levels were severely hit by drought. Each of these problems recurred, and will continue to do so. Yet, there were also specific social and political dimensions to these crises. Thus, in 2004, the deaths of old people through heat-related conditions reflected in part the poor state of governmental care for the elderly, as well as the breakdown of social cohesion, as adult children left the responsibility for their aged parents to the state and, instead, went on holiday. The health system, of which the French were justly proud, did not extend to the long-term care required for effective social welfare. A marked rise in the number and percentage of the elderly was also highly significant, a rise that continues to be the case and is particularly apparent in the small towns of rural France. At the same time, France has played a role in seeking to tackle climate change, notably in pushing for cuts in emissions. It played a role in the Tokyo and Paris climate accords, that of Paris in 2016 being a worldwide agreement to fight global warming.

Alongside its wider international activity, France continued to play a key part in the EU and to be a major beneficiary from it. In 2001, France received 22 per cent of CAP (farm-support) subsidies, and, in 2002, ignoring a critical Britain, reached a bilateral agreement with Germany over the future of the CAP, leaving it unchanged, which then became the basis of EU policy. Far from preserving a way of life, the subsidies in large part bolstered the already most prosperous and productive sections, which more generally was a key aspect of French political economy. The large cereal producers of the prairies of the Île-de-France and Poitou, and the intensive poultry and pork farmers of the west, benefited in particular. A guaranteed market, and the certainty of high prices, provided the security for mechanization and the large-scale use of chemical fertilizers, both aspects of what were increasingly agri-businesses, rather than farms. The EU was superimposed on the existing situation of the state as a system of benefit, and the terms of this in each context provided a matter of contention. There was certainly benefit to be seen in Strasbourg, in its restaurants, and in the Modernist European Parliament buildings opened in 1999.

Despite the support of the CAP, much of French agriculture proved uncompetitive. Indeed, there was a disjuncture between the heavily subsidized large-scale agri-businesses, which were able to compete with the United States in world markets, and small-scale producers who increasingly went bankrupt in the face of over-production and the difficulties of making a viable profit at this scale. The role of the farmer remained important, but the number of farms fell from about 1.6 million in 1970 to about 700,000 in 2005, and the process continues. As president, Chirac, who had earlier been minister of agriculture, very much identified with his rural constituency in the Corrèze, and presented the countryside in terms of an immutable Frenchness. His museum is at Sarran. In contrast, Sarkozy, 'Mr Bling' to the critical media, conspicuously lacked rural interests and (with Hungarian Protestant, Greek Jewish and French Catholic antecedents) had an opulent and cosmopolitan image that was different to traditional concepts of Frenchness. Where Chirac was an assiduous and knowledgeable attender of the annual Paris agricultural show, the Salon International de l'Agriculture, the media delighted in showing a visiting Sarkozy ill at ease among the animals.

A different France was on offer with the southern extension of the TGV service to Marseille in 2001, which led to an expression of the social differentiation of the period, one in which earlier divisions were seen afresh in new forms and also remoulded. Big out-of-town stations on the new line were built to serve Avignon and Aix, ensuring that these cities developed a new relationship with Paris. Wealthy Parisians acquired second homes, either in the cities, especially in their attractive old quarters, leading to socially divisive urban regeneration, or in the surrounding countryside. Prices were driven up, hitting local purchasers keen to acquire property. Being out-of-town, the new stations were particularly convenient to those living in the surrounding countryside; instead of the train being a central feature of urban life with the station in the city centre, it became a key intermediary between the outer-town and the wider world, and served the social dynamics of commuters and second-home owners.

At the same time, the publicly funded rail system saw historic patterns continue, and lines in rural and upland areas used by relatively few were sustained, as in central France, although, from the 2000s, there was strong pressure from within the industry challenging their maintenance. This pressure was in part driven by regulation and the drive for uniformity, for safety requirements ensured the need for significant investment if many of these lines were to remain open. Tourists were more apt to note the spectacular aspects of the transport system, whether the opening of the Channel Tunnel (1992) or, more dramatically, the road bridge across the deep Tarn valley (2004), a bridge that is higher than the Eiffel Tower. The ability to travel by rail at high speed across France certainly contrasted with the situation in Britain and the United States, and was one of which the French were justifiably proud, as well as reducing the pressure on road and air links.

The amalgam of regional economies continued to develop at different rates and there was significant regional change. The decline in long-established industrial communities in the north, notably in the Nord, Pas-de-Calais and Lorraine, continued as once great industrial powerhouses, such as Lille and Roubaix, became the settings for derelict factories, disused coalmines and considerable poverty. So also with the Meuse iron industry, while the Lorraine steel industry faced fresh problems in 2008, and the industrial role of Clermont-Ferrand was hit as Michelin cut its workforce. In contrast, the Rhône-Alpes region saw industrialization, as with electronics near Grenoble. So also with aerospace in Toulouse. Jobs led to domestic migration from the north, where cities such as Reims had only modest population growth, to the south. Profitable service industries became more important, such as insurance in Niort. Yet, more than regionalism was at play, for old-established industries also declined in the south, west and centre, for example papermaking at Angoulême, ceramics at Limoges, coal at Alès and armaments at Saint-Étienne.

Meanwhile, the French population grew to 65.27 million in 2020, in contrast to the trend in some parts of Europe. The government actively pursues pro-natalist policies, and has long regarded it as normal to do so. Partly as a result, the birth rate is above that in Germany, Italy and Spain, and France's population is due to match that of Germany by about 2050, both being approximately 72 million. However, its success is in large part a product of the higher immigrant, especially Algerian, birth rate, rather than that of the 'native' French. By 1993, children born to legally resident immigrants made up 10.8 per cent of the population. That, however, does not capture the impact, as nationality is automatically obtained by children of foreign-born parents on reaching the age of majority, and the children of naturalized foreigners are also citizens. In 2008, it was claimed that about 19 per cent of the population, some 11.8 million people, was made up of foreign-born immigrants and their immediate descendants. By 2016, there were 5.7 million Muslims in France, making up over 8 per cent of the population, although there was no section for religion on the census form and thus figures are approximate. Moreover, immigrants, both legal and illegal, but especially the latter, congregated in the cities, and that increased the sense in rural France of an alien presence. Strong concentrations included Belleville in Paris, the poverty-struck northern districts of Marseille and the North African quarter of Perpignan.

Immigration and immigrant communities were seen as a problem, notably on the Right, and were the targets of legislation and would-be legislation, as by Charles Pasqua, the minister of the interior within Chirac governments from 1986 to 1988 and 1993 to 1995. The 2004 ban on prominent religious symbols in state schools and other public buildings, designed to stop the wearing of the Muslim headscarf and veil, was intended to ensure integration as well as for political advantage, and became a long-term issue, one that played out in localities as well as the politics of the centre. The riots in the *banlieues* (city suburbs) in 2005 made the question of assimilation more prominent, as did the decision by the Conseil d'État in 2008 that applications for nationality should be rejected on the grounds of 'lack of assimilation'. In 2016, Manuel Valls (b. 1962), the prime minister, described Islam as a problem.

Public sensitivity was not restricted to North African immigrants, although it very much focused on Algerians. Hostility toward the prospect of workers from eastern Europe in France at the time of the 2005 referendum on the proposed European constitution indicated the continued public understanding of Europe as an amalgam of national segments, each with different interests, rather than as a common European society. France was less willing than the Blair government of Britain to take in large numbers of immigrants from eastern Europe.

ON THE EVENING OF 15 APRIL 2019 the world looked on in horror as the Cathedral of Notre-Dame, 'Our Lady of Paris', caught fire while under repair. The fire quickly spread to the cathedral's ribbed roof, made up of centuries-old oak

beams, until, at 7.57 p.m., the spire collapsed onto part of the
cathedral's vaulted transept with firefighters rushing to try to
save the rest of the building. The Gothic cathedral, which had
stood on the Île de la Cité for 850 years, seen Napoleon crowned
in 1804 and provided the setting for Victor Hugo's great novel
The Hunchback of Notre-Dame (1831), burned for almost fifteen
hours. As President Macron said afterwards, 'it is the cathedral
of all the French people, even those who have never set foot in it.
Her story is our story and she is burning.'

As a result of the higher birth rate, the median age in 2006 was
thirty-nine, compared to forty-two in Germany and Italy, while
22 per cent of the population was over sixty, compared to 26 per
cent in the other two countries. Yet France served much of the
young badly, with the labour market being poor and inflexible.
The high social charges attached to employees, and the difficulties
and costs of dismissing workers – which therefore made it less
appealing to hire them – tended to encourage investment in
labour-saving machinery. Indeed, there was a marked contrast
between the private sector, which tended to have high productivity,
and the state sector, where productivity was lower and labour
relations worse. The issue of productivity was accentuated by
those of the length of the working week and pensions, both of
which discouraged the hiring of new workers. Despite virtue
signalling, the trade unions were more concerned about conditions
for employees than the plight of the unemployed. Successive presidents sought to address the issue of economic rigidities, but found
that their advocacy had scant impact on trade unionists and only
limited support from the public as a whole. The question of gen-
erational fairness was linked to the size of the provision for
pensions, which in 2019 amounted to 14 per cent of GDP, compared with an Organisation for Economic Co-operation and

Development (OECD) average of 8 per cent, a contrast in part due to the retirement age of sixty-two. Mass protests in 1995, 2003, 2010 and 2019–20 hit plans for pension reform. At the same time, social inequality was accentuated by an emphasis on consumption taxes rather than wealth ones.

With political tension frequently linked to immigration and to related cultural issues, which helped focus the concerns and energies of the *Front national*, critics sought to link this to fascistic Right-wing populist movements prior to the Second World War and to Vichy. There was, indeed, a degree of linkage, but there were also separate concerns, including a widespread sense of alienation from dominant social trends, and not always expressed differently on the Left and Right of the political spectrum. There was disenchantment across the spectrum, but centre-Right governments (Chirac, Sarkozy), centre-Left ones (Hollande) and centre ones (Macron) all sought to mobilize political support and define purpose by presenting themselves as moderate and as bringing the country together accordingly. This stance, however necessary, proved a weak political resource as the popularity of these governments was precarious and, based essentially on an appeal against the extremes, their ability to move policy forward was limited. Thus, the pathology of French politics was not so much the popularity of the *Front national*, serious and disturbing as that is, but, rather, the difficulty of energizing a majority to support reforming policies that could command widespread support. The power of the presidency, as well as electoral victory, gave Macron the initiative, bringing together the triumph of the executive over the legislature in the Fifth Republic, and the prestige of the court element, albeit an ambiguous prestige, as seen with the unpopularity of Macron's frequent staging of events in Versailles. His vulnerability was apparent in the winter of 2019–20; but so also was the essential irrelevance of the Right-wing *Républicains*, the successor to the Gaullists, as well as the negativity of the Left.

15. Conclusions

Conservatism, in large part in protection of vested interests, is a lasting theme in French history, with economic conservatism a key aspect that has lasted to the present. Thus, in the important flour-milling industry prior to the Revolution, millers opposed the combination of mills into larger units which would have reduced costs; bakers hindered changes in milling methods that limited their freedom of action and were reluctant to adapt to new sorts of grain that required different handling, kneading and baking techniques; and the public authorities resisted changes in milling that might lead to popular disquiet. By prohibiting the introduction of certain practices, such as grain purchase on speculation, the authorities impeded the capitalist modernization of the industry. In the modern era, there is similar conservatism, including much rigidity in the labour market. This has been a direct problem for the government. In 2006, five million workers, about a quarter of the workforce, were in the public sector. Consequently, the Sarkozy government's attempt in 2007 to extend the period necessary for worker contributions before full pensions were paid led to debilitating strikes. Popular attitudes to economic activity and its social context proved resistant to government policy, and this resistance was shown in the widespread commitment to getting someone else to pay the bill, including subsidizing one's job. Yet, deregulation was not always as pronounced and controversial as it had been during the Barre ministry (1976–81), and privatizations brought a measure of deregulation, as in the late 1980s and mid-1990s. In 2005, over five million of the population were happy to become shareholders when Électricité de France was partly privatized. Nevertheless, repeated opposition to pension reform reflects both a reluctance to accept change, especially to existing privileges, and the existence of a revolutionary spirit that is directed against government.

Another example of French conservatism is the longstanding emphasis on national distinctiveness. Legislation of 1975 and 1994 banned the use of foreign words in official documents, advertising and packaging, if there were French alternatives. These bans were an indication of a mixture of hubris, stubbornness and lack of confidence. A resistance to the cultural aspects of trade liberalization was clear, with much energy devoted to subsidizing the film industry, and to resisting American cuisine, and American culture more generally. Yet, despite plentiful criticism of Coca-colonization and McDonaldization, 'le Happy Meal' has been very popular from the 2000s, while pasta has been very popular for a very long time, and, in 2014, thanks to rising consumption from 2006, 87 per cent of French adults ate pasta, rice or noodles at least once weekly, the young being particularly prone to do so. Disneyland Paris is one of France's major tourist sites, and the speaking of English has become more common. The strength of both cosmopolitanism and xenophobia have contributed to the sense of flux over identity.

Visitors can readily note changes. Café and restaurant culture was transformed with the prohibition of smoking in 2007. France became one of the inside-out societies, with its fourteen million smokers leaving offices or restaurants in order to 'light up' outside on the public space of the pavement, and the visual character of French culture was changed as public smoking ceased to be regarded as stylish. Other one-time defining characteristics of French culture appear less striking than in the past; this is especially true of Christianity, which has a much weaker hold on French life than in the 1950s. The impact of large-scale Muslim immigration is a factor. So also is a degree of secularism, as well as the individual and collective moral choices and practices involved in divorce, abortion, single parenthood, homosexuality, and couples choosing to live together while unmarried. France has changed alongside the rest of the West, with style and character as well as depression and dissension.

The building and fortune of the state is an obvious narrative for any history of France but, far from being inevitable, change has been in part incremental and largely determined by circumstance and contingency. Alongside violence, the French state, like others, emerged through a process of constantly renegotiated compromises between rulers and ruled. A political system founded in practice on consent as much as the pretensions of authority proved durable and, on the whole, flexible; although with serious lapses in both. The extent of compromise necessary in order to end the Wars of Religion in the 1590s is an aspect of politics that still resonates today. There is a tendency in considering France to focus on its symbols of power and authority, which are, indeed, impressive, and this is the case whether we are looking at President Macron's 'Jupiter'-style presidency or the settings and lifestyles of those officials who wielded authority in the regions. The state's officials have taken over the attributes of authority formerly wielded by the monarchy, and appear very much to enjoy this stance. However, the reality of power and authority are somewhat different, and, in particular, there is an inherent process of compromise, which is part of the trade-off that always really underlay royal power and that has been translated to its republican successor.

Compromise is less commonly a matter now of religion, although, as 1984 was to show, the situation proved different in the case of Church schools, an issue that had a resonance from the Third

Republic, and notably so from the early 1900s. It is unlikely that there will be a comparable compromise in the case of Islam: however elliptically, there is a parallel between Islam and former Christian heterodox movements. Thus, Henry IV's remark 'Paris is worth a mass' no longer has a resonance, but the situation in the 1590s has a different bearing as far as politics today is concerned. Moving from violence, which was the means of politics in that period, to the realities of dissidence and compromise captures much of the situation today. The contexts of presidential activity are very different, but the underlying situation remains the same, and notably so in the need for skill in assuaging anger and creating an appearance of success sufficient to cope with the pressures on power. Henry IV proved to have the necessary skills, ranging from military to political, and in 1598, he brought to a close a sustained crisis. However, all the elements of difficulty remained in play, and, as in other countries, crisis surmounted proved also to be crisis postponed.

It is necessary to be cautious about seeing linear developments or accepting singular explanations about royal or state power. For example, rather than the state becoming necessarily stronger with time, the situation has been more varied. Another instance of the problems associated with unilinear progressivism – trying to find a single direct line through the course of history – is provided by the changing nature of goals, a point exemplified by the Revolution but not limited to it. In his novel *L'An 2440* (1770), Louis-Sébastien Mercier looked forward to regulated wheat production, adequate grain stockpiling, and the improvement of crops and livestock by hybridization and selective breeding. The emphasis today might be more tilted toward environmental concerns but, by 2100, rapid population growth might push the stress back towards production.

The nature of authority and power has always varied within France. In part, this reflects practical limitations, notably in terms of distance, terrain and cover. But, the ideological factor is also highly significant. Here the key ideology is that of the *pays*, and notably so for regions with a strong, separate identity. An important form of conservatism is provided by their continued pull. The region was given a new constitutional and political formulation under the Fifth Republic, one in line with the role of regional politics in the EU as a whole. While the contrasting topographies of particular *pays* remained readily apparent, at the same time there was an erosion of differences in the form of the spread, from the nineteenth century, of a more uniform consumer culture, a process that has greatly escalated since the 1970s. The interplay of country and region indeed remains an important dynamic in French history. Although under French rule for over 250 years, this is the case with Corsica, and Brittany has been the source of much opposition to central government and its regional manifestations over the last decade. Elderly Bretons still speak of having gone 'into France'. The sense of a determination to keep central government at a distance is also the case with regions that appear to the cursory visitor to be less 'different'.

One source of contrast was between frontier regions and others, with the frontier not only physical, but also a border zone of contested state authority as seen with smuggling. Thus, troops were used against smugglers in Dauphiné, including in the 1730s, and Brittany, including in the 1760s, but could achieve relatively little in the absence of local support. This was the case in Roussillon in the 1770s, handicapping both officials and troops, and making it impossible to pursue bands in the interior. However, the regional and linguistic diversity of France was not simply a matter of border zones. Alongside the deliberate suppression of regional languages and cultures, the nineteenth-century republican narrative of one nation was an undoubted perversion of a messy reality reflecting the always imperfect and often forced union of the regions, which had once been independent duchies.

The drive for uniformity met repeated opposition, language being a key battleground. In 1539, by the Edict of Villers-Cotterêts, Francis I determined that only French should be used for official documents, which very much downgraded the range of other languages employed in his dominions. Similarly, the Jacobins sought in 1794 to purge the language of regional dialect or *patois*, as they saw the divisiveness of France's linguistic inheritance as a source of weakness in the patriot project. In Brittany in the 1930s, pupils who spoke only Breton at home had a slate marked with a B tied to their neck at school until they learned French. People, however, continued resisting this process and Occitan, Breton, Basque, Corsican and Alsatian identities are currently riding a wave, although language is not the sole factor.

If the regional theme has been one of the longstanding continuities of French history, another has been that of France within Europe, which has been a matter of cultural links and identity, notably Christianity, as much as war. First united as a result of conquest by Rome, France, in turn, defined its limits by conflicts that lasted until 1945. Yet, there has also been influence, indeed power, through other means, including the varied forms of soft power. The shock of defeat in the Second World War and the challenge of the Cold War led France into a major interest in multilateralism, notably with NATO and what became the EU, but the former has not served France's interests as well as its governments would have liked, and that has led to a distancing, whether de Gaulle leaving the military alliance, or Macron in 2019 claiming that NATO was experiencing 'brain death'. In contrast, an emphasis on the EU has been a favourite of Fifth Republic presidents, and notably of Macron who, in 2017, pressed for a Eurozone budget and advanced the idea of a 'multi-speed Europe', with France a key player in the core region. The course of France's trajectory within Europe remains uncertain. In large part, this uncertainty can be seen as a consequence of the lack of clarity about the likely development of the European project, not least in the face of the resilience of nationalism. Alongside earlier interest as well, French governments from the 1940s have invested heavily in this project, and for ideological as well as political reasons. Nevertheless, it should not be assumed that over the long term, and, in particular, if economic circumstances deteriorate, the cause of Euro-convergence will serve political groups concerned with distinctive senses of national interest and identity, including those in France.

The past can appear to recur, which is very apparent when assessing some of the ideas and differences at play in the current 'culture wars' of French politics. The boom of the 1950s, the modernization of the 1960s and the peaceful transition to socialism in 1981 had led to a measure of confidence that long-established divisions, stemming in their vigour from the French Revolution, had abated. That optimism over social peace looks less pertinent in light of the resurgence of the far-Right, which, however much a minority, is not marginal. Moreover, the eventual unpopularity of governments of the Right (Chirac, Sarkozy), Left (Hollande) and centre (Macron) suggests that the idea of a clear French route that is resisted only by extremists is one that is fraught with difficulties. There is both a revolutionary spirit that leads to problems in governing France and also a love of '*démocratie directe*', as was shown with the 'yellow vests'. This is an old French political tradition.

Some of these longstanding differences can be relocated to particular *pays*. Thus, the degree of Protestantism in specific areas can be related to later republicanism and radicalism, and vice versa. Yet, there has also been considerable success in creating not only a sense of Frenchness, but also one that was implemented and incorporated across what had been a very diverse country. At the cost of a history as difficult as it could be glorious, the country became a nation.

SELECTED FURTHER READING

Any reading list poses the problems of omission and commission, and can date rapidly. To ease that, the focus here is on recent works: earlier ones can be pursued through their reading lists. A more subtle problem, one readily apparent from the direction of this book, is that the overwhelming bulk of the literature takes French history, its direction and almost its inevitability as if it were as a given. In particular, there is a weakness in charting alternative courses for the French regions. I begin deliberately with the geography, not because I favour determinism, but due to its significance.

Geography

Braudel, F., *The Identity of France*, New York, 1988–90

Clout, H., *Themes in the Historical Geography of France*, St Louis, 1977

de Planhol, X., *An Historical Geography of France*, Cambridge, 2006/*Géographie Historique de la France*, Paris, 1989 (if one book deserves attention, it is this)

General Works

Fenby, J., *The History of Modern France*, London, 2015

Hazareesingh, S., *How the French Think*, London, 2015

Price, R., *A Concise History of France*, Cambridge, 2005 (2nd edn)

France to 410 CE

Bourdier, F., *Préhistoire de France*, Paris, 1967

Drinkwater, J. F., *Roman Gaul: The Three Provinces*, New York, 1983

Pigott, S., Daniel, G. and McBurney, C. (eds), *France Before the Romans*, Park Ridge, NJ, 1973

Roman, D., *Histoire de la Gaule*, Paris, 1997

Medieval France

Bull, M., *France in the Central Middle Ages, 900–1200*, Oxford, 2002

Delort, R., *La Vie au Moyen Âge*, Paris, 1982

Gaposchkin, M., *The Making of Saint Louis: Kingship, Sanctity and Crusade in the Later Middle Ages*, Ithaca, NY, 2008

James, E., *The Origins of France: From Clovis to the Capetians 500–1000*, New York, 1982

Potter, D. (ed.), *France in the Later Middle Ages, 1200–1500*, Oxford, 2003

1494–1598

Holt, M. P. (ed.), *Renaissance and Reformation France, 1500–1648*, Oxford, 2002

Knecht, R., *Francis I*, Oxford, 1982

de Muchembled, R., *Sociétés, cultures et mentalités dans la France moderne, XVIe–XVIIIe siècle*, Paris, 2001

1598–1715

Bergin, J., *Cardinal Richelieu*, New Haven, CT, 1990

Mansel, P., *King of the World: The Life of Louis XIV*, London, 2019

Pitts, V. J., *Henri IV of France*, Baltimore, 2008

Shennan, J. H., *The Bourbons*, London, 2007

1715–1788

Hardman, J., *The Life of Louis XVI*, New Haven, CT, 2016

Jones, C., *The Great Nation*, Harmondsworth, 2003

1789

Crook, M. (ed.), *Revolutionary France*, Oxford, 2002

Doyle, W., *The Oxford History of the French Revolution*, Oxford, 2003 (2nd edn)

Price, M., *The Fall of the French Monarchy*, London, 2002

Scurr, R., *Fatal Purity: Robespierre and the French Revolution*, New York, 2006

1799–1815

Alexander, R. S., *Napoleon*, London, 2001

Roberts, A., *Napoleon the Great*, London, 2014

1815–1914

Begley, L., *Why the Dreyfus Affair Matters*, New Haven, CT, and London, 2010

Bresler, F., *Napoleon III*, New York, 1999

Démier, F., *La France du XIX siècle*, Paris, 2000

Mansel, P., *Louis XVIII*, London, 2005 (2nd edn)

Price, M., *The Perilous Crown: France between Revolutions*, London, 2007

Tombs, R., *France 1814–1914* (Longman History of France), London, 1996

Tombs, R., *The Paris Commune, 1871*, London, 1999

1914–1945

Agulhon, M., *La République de Jules Ferry à François Mitterrand, 1880–1995*, Paris, 1997

Paxton, R. O., *Vichy France: Old Guard and New Order, 1940–1944*, New York, 2001

Rémond, R., *Le Siècle dernier, 1918–2002*, Paris, 2003

Smith, L., Audoin-Rouzeau, S. and Becker, A., *France and the Great War, 1914–18*, Cambridge, 2003

1945–2020

Badiou, A., *The Meaning of Sarkozy*, London, 2008

Becker, J.-J., *Histoire politique de la France depuis 1945*, Paris, 1998

Gildea, R., *France since 1945*, Oxford, 2002 (2nd edn)

Jackson, J., *A Certain Idea of France: The Life of Charles de Gaulle*, London, 2018

Nester, W. R., *De Gaulle's Legacy: The Art of Power in France's Fifth Republic*, New York, 2014

Short, P., *Mitterrand: A Study in Ambiguity*, London, 2013

Sirinelli, J.-F. (ed.), *La France de 1914 à nos jours*, Paris, 2004

ACKNOWLEDGMENTS

Thinking about all the trips I have made to France, beginning, as a boy navigator, on two long road trips with my father, brings to mind all those with whom, and for whom, I have travelled. The pleasure and interest of tourism there extend to the long academic research trips I repeatedly made to Paris from 1979 to 1989, and to the very many conferences, lectures and academic trips that have led me across the country.

I would like to thank Alice-Catherine Carls, Malcolm Cook, Edward Corp, Charles Coutinho, Bill Doyle, Hervé Drévillon, Alan Forrest, Jacques Fremeaux, Robert Gildea, Alan James, Colin Jones, Jean-Marc Largeaud, Jean-Baptiste Manchon, Dorothée Perring, Michael Rapport, Frédéric Saffroy, Nigel Saul, Maurice Vaisse and Philip Woodfine for commenting on an earlier draft. They are not responsible for any errors that remain, but they have all been helpful and encouraging. Ben Hayes has been a most supportive publisher and Howard Watson his exemplary self as copy editor. It is a great pleasure to dedicate this book to Charles Coutinho, a fine historian. He and I have made podcasts that I have greatly enjoyed, and that offer another invigorating way to approach the past.

ILLUSTRATION CREDITS

Frontispiece Rainer Lesniewski/Alamy Stock Vector; **I** Jerónimo Alba/Alamy Stock Photo; **II** Robert Zehetmayer/Alamy Stock Photo; **III** Bibliothèque nationale de France, Paris; **IV** incamerastock/Alamy Stock Photo; **V** The Metropolitan Museum of Art, New York; **VI** incamerastock/Alamy Stock Photo; **VII** Valery Egorov/Alamy Stock Photo; **VIII** Musée du Louvre, Paris; **IX** Hemis/Alamy Stock Photo; **X** RMN-Grand Palais (musée du Louvre)/Hervé Lewandowski; **XI** Archives Charmet/Bridgeman Images; **XII, XIII** University of Texas Libraries, The University of Texas at Austin; **XIV** Science History Images/Alamy Stock Photo; **XV** dbimages/Alamy Stock Photo; **XVI** President and Fellows of Harvard College; **XVII** Interfoto/Alamy Stock Photo; **XVIII** Shawshots/Alamy Stock Photo; **XIX** Maurice Savage/Alamy Stock Photo; **XX** David Page/Alamy Stock Photo; **XXI** Tim de Waele/Getty Images; **XXII** Henri Bureau/Sygma/Corbis/VCG via Getty Images; **XXIII** Andrew Baumert/Alamy Stock Photo

INDEX